Contents

Introduction   4

Winter into Spring   9

1. Beef Bundle – Beef Cobbler, Creamy Mash, Roasted Carrots   12

2. Souper Douper Bundle – Minestrone Soup with Pangratatto   18

3. Curry Bundle 1 – Kofta Curry, Dosa Pancakes   22

4. Curry Bundle 2 – Chicken Chaap, Vegetable Makhanawala, Crispy Lentil Balls   28

5. French Bundle 1 – Beef Bourguignon, Root Mash, Bread for Dipping   36

6. BBQ Fish Bundle – Hot Smoked Salmon with King Prawns, Potato Salad with Pickled Cucumber, Wye Valley Asparagus   42

7. Fish Bundle – Luxury Fish Pie, Spring Vegetable Medley   48

8. French Bundle 2 – Coq au Vin Blanc, Pasta, Beans and Peas   52

Spring into Summer   55

9. Italian Bundle 1 – Pennoni Giardiniera – Penne with Spinach Fritters   58

10. Italian Bundle 2 – Milanese Chicken, Spaghetti with Tomato and Basil Velouté   60

11. Spanish Bundle – Chicken, Chorizo and White Beans with Manzanilla, Rice with Saffron, Raisins and Parsley   66

12. Veggie Bundle 1 – Ratatouille Provençal Bake with Orzo   70

13. Greek Bundle 1 – Smoked Stuffed Aubergines, Skordalia   74

14. Greek Bundle 2 – Greek Meatballs with Feta, Little Greek Roast Potatoes, Greek Salad Salsa   78

15. Chinese Bundle 1 – Lemon Chicken, Cucumber Salad, Special Fried Rice   84

16. Chinese Bundle 2 – Barbecued Char Sui Pork with Sticky Sauce, Asian Shredded Noodle Salad with Mango Relish, Spring Onion and Sesame Flat Bread   88

17. Asian Bundle – Asian Poached Chicken, Prawn and Sesame Toasts   96

18. Veggie Bundle 2 – Courgette, Olive and Feta Filo Tart, Tomato Salad with Herbes de Provence   100

Summer into Autumn   105

19. BBQ Bundle – Hot Smoked Barbecued Beef with Chilli Sauce, Brazilian Slaw   108

20. Italian Bundle 3 – Lasagne al Forno, Focaccia with Wild Garlic Pesto   112

21. Southern Bundle 1 – Southern Fried Chicken, Mac 'n' Cheese   120

22. Southern Bundle 2 – Creole Jambalaya, Cheesy Cornbread   124

23. Moroccan Bundle – Lamb Tagine, Rice and Lentil Pilaf   130

24. Middle Eastern Bundle – Lamb Kibbeh, Orange, Carrot, Pickled Onion and Mint Salad 134

Desserts 139

Key Lime Pie 140

Chocolate Cheesecake with Praline Crumb 142

Rose Meringue with Summer Fruits 144

Salted Bourbon and Caramel Pudding 146

Limoncello Meringe Pie 148

Annmarie's Limoncello 150

Baked Goodies 153

Spicy Sausage and Chorizo Rolls 154

Little Chicken and Ham Pies 156

Fudge and Pecan Cookies 158

Quotes from Our Customers 160

Dedication and Thanks 161

Introduction

We moved into our new house in Cardiff in February with a couple of months' renovations ahead of us. My daughter Olivia also joined us, relocating from London.

We stayed with my sister-in-law, Vivian, who kindly offered to put us up whilst the first essential phase of building work started. In March, four weeks into the makeover, the country entered into uncertain territory as the Government informed us that we needed to batten down the hatches and go into lockdown. What the reality of this meant for our lives, business and our future was worrying to say the least. Everything changed in an instant, as it did for so many people.

Work life was also set to change dramatically, so I had to get busy, as my increasing concerns would only make things worse. As a cookery school, my business was also in lockdown and the thought of not having a purpose from day to day was almost unbearable. I sat at the little table we had tucked away in the corner of our room and contemplated an idea: to expand the 'goodies' that we had been offering at our 'Saturday Morning Kitchen' and 'Lunch Club' events. I drew up our first menu of 'bundles' (a selection of beautiful dishes that would go together nicely) and introduced the first menu via an email campaign to our lovely customers. Olivia and I crossed our fingers and toes and waited for the magic to happen. Then the phone rang, then again, and it did not stop! We needed Pam, our ace organiser, to ensure this high demand was deftly managed from the comfort of her home, and the team was forged.

We were literally blown away by the response and as the seriousness of COVID-19 gripped the nation, so the orders each week soared and our Cookery School became a fully operational production kitchen. Our bundles were inspired by a global melting pot of classic recipes. I felt people needed to indulge a little at a time when so much was restricted; to treat themselves and have something delicious to look forward to.

As the weeks progressed, we got to know our customers more and more from a distance. Their kind words meant so much to us, we had no idea what our weekly efforts meant to them. We received emails of gratitude, gifts of flowers and chocolates, even homemade limoncello! It was clear that people were missing their daily social interaction, the freedom

of popping out to their favourite restaurant, or dining with friends and family at home. We were delighted to learn that our food meant Friday nights had become date nights for some, others used Zoom to have a virtual supper party with our food, whilst some brought treats to share with other family members, friends and neighbours. It felt so special for us to be able to do this under such difficult circumstances.

One difficulty was getting ingredients. Flour had become as scarce as hen's teeth and items like pasta were rationed. Luckily, we found a brilliant supplier, the World Food Shop, that had these items and so much more in abundance. It became our new favourite place to shop. We also had amazing suppliers, including the aptly named Matt Fresh, who brought us beautiful seasonal fruit, vegetables and herbs, as well as helping out with dairy produce. We got to know Matt well and the laughs we shared each morning were a tonic. Like many small businesses, he had to reinvent himself. Restaurants and hotels were closed, so he turned his hand to offering home deliveries, which were essential for those self-isolating, and so he was able to continue the good work. It was much the same for our butcher and fishmonger.

I have to pay homage to my daughter, Olivia, who found her feet very quickly by my side and soon became my right hand in the kitchen. I feel proud that she has turned such a challenging time into a positive one. We have forged plans for the future and are excited. Surely that's odd at a time like this, but we believe there are better times ahead and that we can work through the difficulties we face.

As I write this, we are entering a second phase of lockdown restrictions and we plan to continue to provide our weekly bundles. This book features a collection of some of the best-loved bundles from the past year and is dedicated to all those who have asked for the recipes.

Our hope is that you, and many others who are eager to create a great 'at home dining experience', can draw inspiration from this recipe collection, beautifully photographed by Huw Jones and designed and published by Graffeg. It is food for the soul and we all need a little of that from time to time, especially now.

Wishing you many happy culinary adventures.

Angela

We hope you enjoy cooking our recipes. They start in season from the end of winter through to autumn. We have put our store cupboard to great use, mixing flavour blends with fresh ingredients. We have also used the barbecue and smoker to add flavour to some dishes as well as brining and marinating. All these methods are classic and you will find yourself learning new tricks as you work your way through the book.

Some recipes may seem a little daunting, as they contain lists of ingredients, but just get yourself organised and the preparation and cooking is a joy, not to mention the eating. Have fun!

Winter into Spring

Souper
Douper
Bundle

Beef Bundle

Beef Cobbler, Creamy Mash and Roasted Carrots

Ingredients

500g trimmed slow cook cut of beef e.g. shin, chuck, or blade

Seasoning

2 flat teaspoons sea salt, ¼ teaspoon black pepper, 1 flat teaspoon garlic granules, 1 flat teaspoon dried thyme, ½ teaspoon sugar. Mix in a pestle and mortar if you have one

1 tablespoon plain flour

Sunflower oil for frying

1 large onion, peeled and finely diced

200g smoked pancetta, diced

2 celery sticks, trimmed, peeled, and sliced

2 large carrots, peeled and roughly chopped

4 cloves garlic, peeled and sliced

150g button mushrooms, wiped and sliced

2 stems of fresh thyme

2 bay leaves

300ml fruity red wine e.g. Merlot

500ml beef stock ("Baxters" Beef Consommé is brilliant!)

Sea salt and black pepper

To thicken and flavour

1 dessertspoon of plain flour

1 heaped teaspoon Dijon mustard

1 dessertspoon Worcestershire sauce

1 teaspoon tomato purée

Scone Topping

450g self-raising flour

1 tablespoon of baking powder

120g salted butter

½ teaspoon sea salt

150g extra mature cheddar or Gruyère cheese, grated

100ml soured cream (I buy a small pot and use the rest to dot on top of the finished cobbler)

150ml milk (you may not need it all)

1 medium egg, beaten with 1 tablespoon of water, for glazing

2 tablespoons of chopped herbs, such as parsley, chives, thyme, tarragon; a little mix up of two or three together is delicious

Serves 4

What you do

1 Mix all the seasoning ingredients for the beef and add the flour, mixing well. Coat all the pieces of beef with the seasoned flour, reserving any excess flour for the sauce.

2 Heat 4 tablespoons of sunflower oil in a large skillet/frying pan and brown the beef pieces in 3 batches, making sure they sizzle as soon as they hit the oil and are lightly browned all over. Remove with a slotted spoon and place in a casserole/gratin dish.

3 At this point, check the oil to make sure any sediment from cooking is not burnt; if it is, wipe out the pan and add 2 tablespoons of fresh oil. If the beef oil is OK, then just continue cooking with it.

4 Add the onion, pancetta, celery and carrot and stir through. Cover with a lid and sweat for a good 7-10 minutes, stirring occasionally. You should have a good medium sizzle sound going on all the time.

⑤ Next, add the garlic, mushrooms, thyme stems and bay leaves and stir through, scraping up any sticky juices from the pan. Now add the wine and use this to dissolve/deglaze any sticky bits – this is fabulous natural flavour here!

⑥ Pour in the stock, add the beef and any resting juices into the pan and bring to the boil. Reduce to a slow simmer and pop the lid on. Cook slowly for about 2 hours, or until the meat is beautifully soft. Taste the sauce and adjust if you need to with sea salt and pepper.

⑦ Meanwhile, make the scones. Place the flour, baking powder, butter and sea salt in a food processor and blend to a fine breadcrumb consistency. Add the herbs and three-quarters of the grated cheese and pulse twice to blend in. Add the soured cream and half the milk, pulse to blend and the mixture should start to come together. Add enough of the remaining milk to form a firm but combined dough – not too wet, not too dry.

⑧ Turn the dough out onto a lightly floured surface and bring together into a ball. Place in a bowl, cover with a cloth and leave to rest for 20 minutes.

⑨ Next, thicken the beef. First, discard the thyme and bay, then mix all the ingredients, plus 3 tablespoons of water, to make a smooth paste. Whisk this into the sauce to thicken and add further flavour.

⑩ After resting, tip the dough out onto a lightly floured surface and roll out to about 3.5cm thick. Use a 7cm round cutter to cut out the scones and arrange on top of the beef. Alternatively, keep it rustic and break up even-sized blobs of dough on top. Brush with beaten egg and sprinkle over the remaining cheese.

11 Place the cobbler on a baking sheet and bake in a preheated oven at 170°C/Fan 150°C/Gas 3 for 30-40 minutes or until the scones are deliciously golden.

This dish is one of many featured in the book that benefit from having a pre-seasoning added to the meat. The flavour is deliciously complex and the slow cooking method gives the whole dish a lovely rich finish.

Roasted Carrots

Ingredients

1kg carrots, peeled and cut lengthways

25g butter

2 tablespoons olive oil

2 tablespoons honey

2 tablespoons lemon juice and 1 teaspoon lemon zest

1 tablespoon chopped parsley to finish

Serves 4

What you do

1 Preheat the oven to 200°C/Fan 180°C/Gas 6. Bring a large pan of salted water to the boil. Add the carrots, bring back up to the boil and cook for 5 minutes.

2 Drain the carrots and leave in a colander to steam dry for a few minutes and then toss in a large roasting tin lined with baking parchment. Heat together the butter, olive oil, honey, lemon juice and zest and brush all over the carrots. Roast for 30-40 minutes until lightly golden. Remove and sprinkle with chopped parsley.

Creamy Mash

Ingredients

1kg floury potatoes, such as King Edward or Maris Piper, cut into even chunks

150ml double cream

50g salted butter

¼ teaspoon white pepper

A few scrapes of fresh nutmeg (optional)

Serves 4

What you do

1 Bring a large saucepan of water to the boil with 1 teaspoon of sea salt. Add the potatoes and boil for about 15 minutes or until tender right through. Drain in a colander and then tip the potatoes back into the pan and place over a very low heat for about 2 minutes to dry them out completely. Spoon them into a potato ricer a little at a time and push through into a warmed bowl.

2 Heat the cream, butter, pepper, and nutmeg in a small pan, pour over the potatoes and beat with a wooden spoon. Serve with the beef cobbler and roast carrots.

Minestrone Soup with Pangratatto

Ingredients

2 tablespoons olive oil

3 medium carrots, peeled and cut into small cubes

1 large red onion, peeled and coarsely chopped

2 large sticks celery, trimmed, peeled, and diced

5 large cloves garlic, peeled and grated

300g Swiss chard/cavolo nero or cabbage – chop the central rib/stalks finely and shred the leaves

Small bunch parsley, chopped

400g tinned tomatoes

400g cannellini beans, drained and rinsed

2L good chicken or vegetable stock

75g stelline (little stars) or orzo pasta

Pangrattato

2 tablespoons olive oil

100g breadcrumbs

1 clove garlic, peeled and finely chopped

A few sprigs of thyme and sage

1 teaspoon lemon zest

25g freshly grated Parmesan to serve

Some parsley leaves, chopped

Serves 4

What you do

1 Heat the olive oil in a large saucepan and slowly fry the carrots,

onion and celery until soft and golden. Add a cartouche/foil hat directly on top, plus a lid; this will speed up the cooking. This will take about 15-20 minutes, but it is worth it. The slow cooking gives a lovely richer taste to the finished soup.

2 Stir in the garlic, chopped cabbage/chard/cavolo nero stalks, adding a little water, and stir to prevent sticking. Stir in the tomatoes and cook for 10 minutes or until reduced to a loose paste.

3 Add the beans and cook for a further 5 minutes, then mash them slightly. Pour in the stock and bring to the boil, then reduce the heat and simmer for 30 minutes.

4 Meanwhile, make the pangratatto. Heat the oil in a frying pan over medium heat. Add the breadcrumbs and fry until lightly golden. Stir in the garlic, lemon zest and herbs, cook for 1 minute, then remove from the heat. Once cool, stir in the Parmesan.

5 To finish the soup, add the pasta followed by the shredded greens leaves and blanch briefly so they remain green and crisp. Cook until the pasta is soft; they both take the same amount of time. If the consistency of the soup is too thick, add a little water.

6 Season when slightly cooled, stir in the parsley and serve hot with pangratatto sprinkled over the top.

This can be a pure vegetable/vegan soup, just use vegetable stock in place of chicken and use a vegan cheese in place of Parmesan.

Curry Bundles

Kofta Curry

Ingredients

For the meatballs

1 small onion, peeled and roughly chopped

1 medium green chilli, split and roughly chopped

2 tablespoons fresh chopped coriander

1 tablespoon mint leaves, chopped

4 cloves garlic, finely chopped

1 tablespoon finely chopped ginger

450g mined beef or lamb with some fat, not too lean

2 tablespoons gram/chickpea flour

1 medium free-range egg, lightly whisked

1 teaspoon freshly squeezed lemon juice

1 teaspoon cumin powder

1 teaspoon fresh ground coriander

1 teaspoon turmeric powder

½ teaspoon fresh ground black pepper

½ teaspoon Kashmiri chilli powder

1 teaspoon garam masala

1 rounded teaspoon sea salt

For the curry

4 tablespoons sunflower oil

1 large onion, peeled and finely chopped

2 medium tomatoes, roughly chopped

1 green medium chilli, split and finely chopped

1 teaspoon cumin seeds

3 whole cloves

1-inch cinnamon stick

1 bay leaf

1-2 green cardamom pods, split

4-5 cloves garlic, finely chopped

1 thumb-tip-sized piece of ginger, scraped and chopped

3 tablespoons whole milk Greek yoghurt

1 teaspoon fresh ground cumin

1 teaspoon fresh ground coriander

½ -1 teaspoon Kashmiri chilli powder

½ teaspoon turmeric powder

1 teaspoon sweet paprika

1½ teaspoon sea salt

500ml water or vegetable stock

1 teaspoon garam masala

2 tablespoons fresh chopped coriander to finish

Serves 4

What you do

1 **For the meatballs –** Put the onion, green chilli, coriander leaves and mint leaves into a food processor. Use the pulse function to combine so that the onions are finely chopped but not blended and watery, then add the rest of the ingredients listed for the meatballs and process to combine for about 30 seconds until well mixed and smooth. Lightly oil your hands and form about 25 meatballs. Set aside.

1 **For the curry sauce –** Clean your food processor bowl, add the onion for the curry sauce and use the pulse function again to chop the onion. Remove and set aside. Add the tomatoes and chilli to the processor and chop together, remove and set aside.

2 Heat a large heavy-bottomed pan over high heat. Add the sunflower oil and whole spices (1 teaspoon cumin seeds, 3 whole cloves, 1-inch cinnamon stick, 1 bay leaf, 1-2 green cardamom pods, split) and allow them to sizzle for a few seconds. Add the chopped onion and sauté, stirring often, for 7-8 minutes, or until soft and golden.

3 Lower the heat to medium-high. Add the garlic and ginger and sauté for another 2 minutes until the onions have deepened in colour and are slightly sticky. Add the chopped tomatoes and green chilli mixture, followed by the yoghurt, ground spices and sea salt. Sauté for 4-5 minutes or until the oil starts to separate from the mixture, creating little holes.

4 Pour in the water or stock and raise the heat to bring to a boil. When the water comes to a boil, lower the heat to the lowest setting. Once it has stopped boiling, arrange the meatballs/kofta in a single layer.

5 Raise the heat to medium, cover and allow it to cook for 10 minutes. Uncover and gently stir the kofta. Lower the heat to low-medium. Cover and allow it to simmer for another 35 minutes, stirring once in between, until they are cooked through.

6 Remove the lid and lightly simmer to evaporate the liquid to a nice thickened consistency. Taste and add salt, if needed. Sprinkle in the garam masala and chopped coriander to finish.

We are a nation of curry lovers and during lockdown it was clear that people were missing their regular spice fix, so we offered a weekly curry bundle on our menu using regional inspiration from India. These are some of the favourite bundles.

Dosa Pancakes

Ingredients

100g chickpea/gram flour

100g plain flour

200ml full-fat milk

300ml of cold water

For the masala filling

750g peeled weight of good mashing potatoes e.g. Maris Piper or whites, chopped into small cubes

200g leaf spinach, washed and drained

1 tablespoon butter

2 tablespoons sunflower oil

2 teaspoons black onion/nigella seeds

2 teaspoons fennel seeds

2 teaspoons cumin seeds

1 red chilli, chopped (seeds and membrane removed for a cooler finish)

1 large onion, peeled, halved, and very thinly sliced

4 large garlic cloves, finely grated

1 thumb-top-sized piece of ginger, finely chopped

8 stems of coriander leaves, finely chopped

2 tablespoons fresh curry leaves

1 teaspoon ground turmeric

1 teaspoon fresh ground coriander

100ml water

Coconut Raita

200g fresh grated coconut (available frozen from Indian supermarkets or online)

200ml Greek full-fat yoghurt

A small bunch of coriander, leaves only, finely chopped

1 teaspoon lime zest

1 tablespoon of lime juice

Sea salt to taste

Serves 4

What you do

1 In my experience, the best results for dosa pancakes are achieved if you make the batter a couple of days before and leave it covered in the fridge.

2 Measure the flours into a large bowl and whisk through to break up any lumps in the chickpea flour. Make a well in the centre, pour in the milk and water and season with salt. Whisk to a smooth batter, then cover with cling film and chill for 24 hours or up to 5 days.

3 **To make the filling –** Pop the potatoes in salted water and cook until almost soft through. Drain well. Heat the oven to 200°C/ Fan 180°C/Gas 6. Toss the cooked potatoes in a good drizzle of the oil and spread out on a large baking tray lined with baking parchment. Place in the oven and cook for 20 minutes, stirring on the tray once

or twice during cooking, until they start to brown.

4 Meanwhile, heat the remaining oil in a large frying pan and cook the black onion, fennel, and cumin seeds for 30 seconds or so until fragrant. Stir in the chilli, onion, garlic, ginger, chopped coriander and curry leaves, cook over a low heat for about 10 minutes until the onion is soft. Stir in the ground spices and cook for 15 seconds, then add 100ml water and simmer to bring all the flavours together. Add the spinach leaves with the butter and wilt.

5 Spoon the mixture over the potatoes, season well and mix through, crushing the potatoes slightly creating a chunky mash. Keep the mixture warm until the pancakes are ready (or leave it to cool, then chill for up to 2 days. Gently reheat in the pan or microwave before continuing).

6 **To make the raita –** Pop the grated coconut into a bowl. Stir in

the yoghurt, chopped coriander, lime zest and juice, and a pinch of salt. Cover and chill until ready to serve (you can also make this up to 2 days ahead, but stir in the coriander just before serving).

7 **To cook and assemble the dosa** – Heat the oven to its lowest setting and put a baking sheet inside ready to keep the dosas warm once you have cooked them. If the dosa batter has thickened in the fridge, thin it down a little by adding 2-4 tablespoons of cold water. It should resemble the consistency of double cream.

8 Brush a little oil into a large non-stick frying pan, place over a medium to high heat and once you can feel the heat radiating up over the pan, pour a ladleful of the dosa batter into the centre of the pan and quickly swirl it around to cover the surface, making the pancake as thin as you can. When the surface of the pancake looks almost dry and curls away at the edge of the pan, spoon a quarter of the potato filling down the centre. When the pancake is deep golden brown and crisp on the underside, roll it up in the pan to encase the filling. Cook for a minute more, then transfer to the oven to keep warm while you continue cooking the remaining dosas. Serve with the kofta curry and coconut riata.

Chicken Chaap

Ingredients

Garam masala

½ teaspoon cloves

½ teaspoon black cardamom seeds

1 whole nutmeg

2 pieces mace

6 Indian bay leaves

2 tablespoons coriander seeds

1 heaped teaspoon cumin seeds

2 dried red chillies

5cm soft cinnamon stick

Chicken

¼ teaspoon saffron strands

10 tablespoons sunflower oil

3 large onions, peeled, halved, and sliced very thinly

1.2L full-fat Greek yoghurt

2 tablespoons grated garlic

2 tablespoons finely chopped ginger

6 chicken thigh/leg joints

1 tablespoon ground coriander

2 teaspoons Kashmiri chilli powder

4 level teaspoons sea salt

2 level teaspoons sugar

1 tablespoon toasted flaked almonds to finish

Serves 4

What you do

1 **To make the garam masala** – Put a large frying pan over a medium heat and when hot, add the bashed spices, roast, stirring continuously to prevent them from burning. As soon as the mixture becomes really fragrant, which is about 30 seconds tip into a bowl to cool.

2 Spoon into a spice or coffee grinder and blend to a powder. Keep

in a little clip jar and it will be fresh for about 6 weeks.

③ If using saffron to colour the dish, infuse in a small bowl with 4 tablespoons of tepid water and leave to bleed out the colour.

④ **To caramelise the onions** – This is the secret to the success of this dish, so take your time. Heat 6 tablespoons of the oil in a heavy-based frying pan over a medium-high heat. Pick up a piece of onion and dip the edge into the hot oil, keeping your fingers at a safe distance – the onion should immediately start to sizzle. Add all the onions to the pan, stir gently, then prepare a slotted spoon and plate to one side, ready to drain the onions later.

⑤ Cook until the onions look glossy, add a large pinch of salt, stir through, and continue cooking for a further 20 minutes or so, stirring occasionally so they are evenly cooked to a lovely deep golden brown.

⑥ As soon as the onions are caramelised, drain, pushing the spoon against the side of the pan so that any excess oil remains in the pan. Pop the onions onto a plate and reserve the oil.

⑦ **The sauce** – In a large bowl, mix the yoghurt with the garlic, ginger, 1 tablespoon of the fresh garam masala and the oil saved from the onions.

⑧ Heat the remaining 4 tablespoons of oil in a large pan over a medium-high heat. Add the chicken joints and seal until lightly golden on all sides. Lower the heat to medium and pour the yoghurt mixture over the chicken. Keep the heat at medium so the contents of the pan do not boil.

⑨ Add the caramelised onions and ground coriander and cook, stirring continuously, for 10 minutes.

10 When the oil rises to the surface and the yoghurt splits, add the chilli powder and salt and stir through. Bring the sauce to a boil, then reduce the heat. Add the saffron and juice at this point, mix through and cover, cooking the chicken for a further 20 minutes, stirring occasionally. Add the sugar and stir to mix thoroughly.

11 Before serving, taste the sauce to check the seasoning and adjust as necessary. To serve, garnish with the toasted flaked almonds and a little sprinkle of your garam masala.

There really isn't anything like your own freshly made garam masala and it is easy to make. I pre-bash the spices in a mortar and pestle so they roast evenly and break up nicely in the blender.

Vegetable Makhanawala

Ingredients

Spice Blend

1 heaped teaspoon fresh ground cumin

1 rounded teaspoon fresh ground coriander

1 level teaspoon turmeric

½ -1 teaspoon Kashmiri chilli powder

1 level teaspoon garam masala

1 teaspoon fenugreek

½ teaspoon sugar

Curry base

2 tablespoons sunflower oil

1 small onion, peeled and sliced

1 medium carrot, peeled and diced

2 cloves garlic, peeled and pasted with a little salt

1-inch piece ginger, peeled and finely chopped

2 large tomatoes, finely chopped

10 cashews, crushed to a powder

1 dessertspoon Swiss Marigold vegetable powder

Vegetables

1 red pepper, deseeded and cubed

100g green beans, cut in half

1 small cauliflower, cut into florets

100g peas, fresh/frozen

300ml water or vegetable stock (Marigold Swiss Vegetable Powder is great)

To finish

1 teaspoon tomato purée

1-2 tablespoons lemon juice

3 tablespoons double cream

1 heaped tablespoon chopped coriander

Serves 4

What you do

1 Take a large skillet or chef pan, heat the oil, add the onion and carrot and sauté until soft and starting to colour. Stir in the garlic and ginger, cook for 1 minute, then add the chopped tomatoes, cashew powder and vegetable powder.

2 Add the chopped pepper and continue to sauté. Cover and simmer for 2 minutes. Remove the lid and add the spice blend with salt to taste and cook over a low heat for 2 minutes.

3 Add the water/stock and then the prepared vegetables. Simmer gently for 10-15 minutes until just soft.

4 Add the tomato purée, lemon juice, cream, and coriander to finish the dish.

5 Serve with rice and our lentil balls – they are delicious.

Crispy Lentil Balls

Ingredients

400g chana dhal, rinsed and soaked in water overnight

1 medium onion, peeled and finely chopped

1 green chilli, split, deseeded, and finely chopped

1 red chilli, split, deseeded, and finely chopped

1 rounded teaspoon finely chopped ginger

1 tablespoon tamarind paste

1 teaspoon sugar

1 rounded teaspoon cumin seeds

1 teaspoon garam masala

1 sprig fresh curry leaves

1 teaspoon sea salt

Sunflower oil for frying

Makes about 12 balls

What you do

1 Drain the chana dhal, tip into a food processor and pulse until the mixture has a slightly coarse texture but comes together.

2 Scrape into a mixing bowl and add the finely chopped onion, green and red chillies, ginger, tamarind, sugar, cumin seeds, garam masala, curry leaves and salt. Mix well and taste – the mixture should have a slight sweet and sour finish. Increase the tamarind and sugar if more is needed.

3 Shape the dough into little balls about 5cm/2 inches in diameter.

4 Heat about 2.5cm/1 inch of vegetable oil in a deep saucepan.

5 Gently drop the lentil balls into hot oil over medium-low heat and fry until golden brown, about 3 to 4 minutes. Remove and drain on a metal strainer.

BBQ Fish Bundle

French
Bundle 1

Beef Bourguignon

Ingredients

1 tablespoon extra-virgin olive oil

200g thick bacon or pancetta, roughly chopped

1.2kg beef chuck steak or stewing beef, cut into 10cm/4-inch chunks

1 large carrot, thickly sliced

2 large sticks of celery, peeled and diced

1 large white onion, peeled, halved, and diced

6 cloves garlic, grated

1 teaspoon sea salt and freshly ground pepper

2 tablespoons plain flour

12 small shallots, peeled

1 bottle red wine, such as Merlot, Côte du Rhône, or red Burgundy

700ml good beef stock

2 tablespoons tomato purée

1 beef stock jelly

1 teaspoon fresh thyme, finely chopped

2 tablespoons fresh parsley, finely chopped

2 bay leaves

400g small white or brown mushrooms, quartered

2 tablespoons salted butter

Serves 4

What you do

1 Preheat the oven to 170°C/Fan 150°C/Gas 3.

2 Pour the oil into a large, heavy casserole over a medium heat, add the bacon/pancetta and sauté for about 3 minutes until crisp and browned. Remove onto a plate with a slotted spoon.

3 Pat the beef pieces dry with some paper towel, then add to the pan in batches and sear all over until browned. Remove from the dish and place with the bacon.

4 Now add the carrots, celery, and onions, stir and sauté until softened (about 3 minutes), stir in 4 of the cloves of grated garlic and cook for 1 minute. Drain any excess fat from the pan but leave about 1 tablespoon.

5 Add the bacon and beef, plus any resting juices, back into the pan, seasoning with 1 level teaspoon of sea salt and ¼ teaspoon of ground black pepper. Sprinkle with the flour, mix in well and cook for 4-5 minutes to brown.

6 Add the shallots, wine, and enough stock so that the meat is barely covered, then stir in the tomato paste, jelly stock cube and herbs. Bring to a simmer on the stove.

7 Cover the casserole with a lid, place on the lower shelf of the oven and slow cook for 3 to 4 hours, or until the meat falls apart and is tender.

8 Whilst the beef is cooking, prepare and pre-cook the mushrooms by heating the butter in a medium-sized pan over a medium heat. When it foams, add the remaining 2 cloves of grated garlic and cook until fragrant (about 30 seconds), then add in the mushrooms. Cook for about 5 minutes whilst shaking the pan occasionally to coat with the butter. Season with salt and pepper. Once they are browned, set aside.

9 Add the mushrooms to the beef during the last 15 minutes of cooking.

10 Once the beef is ready, remove from the sauce with a slotted spoon together with the vegetables and herbs. Simmer the sauce, skimming off any additional fat that rises to the surface. If the sauce is a little thin, thicken with 1 heaped teaspoon of cornflour mixed with 2 tablespoons of cold water and gradually add to the sauce whilst stirring. Taste and add a little more sea salt if needed.

11 Pour the meat and vegetables back into the sauce and heat for 3 minutes. Serve with our root mash and some delicious bread to mop up any sauce.

This dish takes me back to my roots and the art of classic French cooking, where you learn so much in the kitchen just from one dish.

Root Mash

Ingredients

300g potatoes, peeled and cubed

300g swede, peeled and cubed

3 medium carrots, peeled and cubed

1 large garlic clove

25g salted butter

1 heaped tablespoon crème fraîche, cream cheese or Greek yoghurt

Sea salt

Black pepper

6 scrapes of nutmeg

Serves 4

What you do

1. Place the potatoes, swede, and carrots in a large pan of salted water. Bring to the boil, add the garlic and cook for 20-25 minutes until everything is tender.

2. Drain well and ideally pass through a potato ricer in batches, or mash with a potato masher. Stir in the butter, crème fraiche, sea salt to taste, pepper, and nutmeg. Whip with a wooden spoon or spatula and serve in a warm bowl or dish.

Bread for Dipping

Ingredients

152g milk

227g lukewarm water

85g salted butter, softened

2 teaspoons fine sea salt

35g caster sugar

50g dried skimmed milk

567g strong bread flour

2 teaspoons fast active yeast

2 tablespoons chopped herbs e.g. thyme, rosemary, parsley

Serves 4

What you do

1 Take a large mixing bowl and add in all of the ingredients, mixing together into a soft dough. Knead by hand, or place in a stand mixer with a dough hook. The finished dough should be smooth in appearance – 10 minutes by hand, 4 minutes by machine.

2 Transfer the dough to a lightly oiled bowl and allow the dough to rise until puffy in appearance and doubled in size – about 1½ hours, depending on the warmth of your kitchen.

3 Lightly oil 2 x 6" rectangle foil containers. Tip the risen dough out onto a lightly oiled surface, shape it into 2 x 6" logs and place each into a foil. Cover with lightly oiled cling film, and allow the dough to rise until it's just below the lip of the

foil – about 45 minutes to 1 hour, depending on the warmth of your kitchen.

④ Preheat the oven to 200°C/Fan 180°C/Gas 6.

⑤ Remove the cling film and place the foils in the oven. Bake the bread for 25 minutes until well risen and golden on top. Remove and decant onto a cooling rack to cool completely. You can re-warm the bread in the foil for 7 minutes at 180°C/Fan 160°C/Gas 4. The bread freezes beautifully.

This is a little Pain de Mie recipe adapted into mini loaves, perfect for mopping up a good sauce and they freeze beautifully.

Hot Smoked Salmon with King Prawns

Ingredients

4 x 150g salmon fillets, skin on

8 large raw tiger prawns, shell on

Brine

2 litres water

160g sea salt

80g sugar

½ teaspoon black peppercorns

2 slices of onion

4 slices lemon

Rub

1 rounded teaspoon sea salt

1 rounded teaspoon pink peppercorns, crushed

½ teaspoon black peppercorns, crushed

1 rounded teaspoon fennel seeds

1 rounded teaspoon garlic cloves

1 teaspoon smoked paprika

1 teaspoon freeze-dried dill

1 teaspoon sugar

Smoke

2 handfuls apple wood chips, soaked

Serves 4

What you do

1 Bring all the ingredients for the brine together in a mixing bowl. Add the fish fillets for 20 minutes, adding the prawns to the bowl after 15 minutes.

2 Drain well and pat dry with kitchen paper.

3 Mix the ingredients together for the rub and sprinkle over the fish fillets and prawns.

4 Place the salmon fillets on a convection tray lined with parchment paper.

5 Set your BBQ to 180-200°C for indirect cooking and place the fish tray along the centre of the grill. Drain the wood chips and divide between each charcoal basket. Pop the lid on and smoke for 10 minutes, then add the prawns quickly and continue smoking and cooking until the prawns turn pink and the fish reaches a temperature of 60°C at the thickest part of the fillet.

6 Remove from the BBQ and cover with a sheet of foil and a tea towel, leaving to rest for 10 minutes.

7 Serve with the potato salad and asparagus.

Barbecuing has become a real passion of mine, the flavours and results you can achieve with this cooking method are stunning. This recipe is simple, but the brining method makes all the difference to the end result. We have therefore used brining in quite a few of our dishes.

Potato Salad with Pickled Cucumber

Ingredients

600g smallish new potatoes

200g cucumber, peeled, deseeded and shredded

2 tablespoons white wine vinegar

1 teaspoon sugar

¼ teaspoon pink peppercorns, crumbled

Dressing

2 tablespoons mayonnaise

1 tablespoon Greek yoghurt or crème fraîche

1 teaspoon Dijon mustard

1 tablespoon capers (optional)

1 tablespoon chopped parsley

1 small red onion, sliced and soaked in 500ml cold water for 20 minutes

Serves 4

What you do

1 Wash the potatoes and trim away any imperfections. Cut any large potatoes in half to even up the sizes.

2 Boil in salted water until soft and drain well.

3 Whilst the potatoes are cooling slightly, mix together the cucumber, white wine vinegar, sugar and pink peppercorns in a bowl. Set aside to cure for 15 minutes.

4 Make the dressing by simply mixing everything together in a large bowl. Drain the onion and squeeze out the excess water, add this to the dressing and stir

through. Once the cucumber has cured for 15 minutes, drain away the excess liquid and add to the dressing.

5 Stir in the warm potatoes and mix well. Cover and chill until needed. Remove from the fridge 40 minutes before serving so the flavours flourish.

Wye Valley Asparagus

We love cooking this on the grill over direct heat from the charcoal on the BBQ.

1 Simply trim the spears at the base, where it is a little woody, brush lightly with a little olive oil, sprinkle with sea salt and freshly ground black pepper and grill for about 5-7 minutes until lightly charred.

Fish
Bundle

French
Bundle 2

Luxury Fish Pie

Ingredients

Béchamel

600ml full-fat milk + a slice of onion, 2 slices of carrot + celery leaf + 2 peppercorns + a bay leaf

50g butter

50g plain flour

1 heaped teaspoon Dijon mustard

¼ teaspoon cayenne or chilli powder (optional)

4 tablespoons double cream

1 tablespoon soft herbs, such as chives, dill, parsley of tarragon

150g leek, sliced thinly

8 little button mushrooms, halved

Filling

350g fish fillet e.g. haddock, hake, coley, ling, cut into cubes

8 tiger prawns

50g smoked salmon, shredded

8 queen scallops

Topping

600g potatoes, peeled and cubed

50g butter

2 tablespoons double cream or crème fraiche

50ml full-fat milk

Sea salt and white pepper to taste

6 scrapes of nutmeg

2 medium free-range eggs, separated

Serves 4

What you do

1 First, make the béchamel. Pour the milk into a saucepan and heat together with the onion, carrot, celery, peppercorns and bay. Cook until near boiling point, remove

from the heat, cover, and leave to cool for 20 minutes.

2 Meanwhile, cook the potatoes in salted water until soft right through, drain well, place in the saucepan and mash or put through a ricer. Add the butter, cream or crème fraiche, milk and season to taste and add the nutmeg. Set aside.

3 To finish the sauce, melt the butter and sauté the leek and mushroom until soft, stir in the flour, Dijon mustard and cayenne pepper if using, then slowly add the flavored milk and the double cream. Stir until thickened and season to taste.

4 Cut the fish into bite-sized chunks and de-head, peel, and de-vein the prawns. Add all the seafood to the sauce and spoon into a medium-sized ovenproof dish.

5 Fold the egg yolk into the potato and whip to combine nicely. Whisk the egg white until stiff and fold into the potato. Spoon the mixture onto the top of the fish mix.

6 Bake in a preheated oven at 190°C/Fan 170°C/Gas 5 for 30 minutes, then 10 minutes at 180°C/Fan 160°C/Gas 4. The top should be richly golden and crisp.

A homage to my lovely mum, Betty, who always made a stunning fish pie. She never skimped on portions, using great chunks of fish and plenty of prawns. It was delicious!

Spring Vegetable Medley

Ingredients

300g baby carrots, scraped and trimmed

200g asparagus spears, trimmed

1 fennel bulb, trimmed and thinly sliced

200g sugar snap peas or mangetout

25g butter

1 tablespoon chopped soft herbs, such as parsley, chives, or tarragon

Serves 4

What you do

1. Bring a large saucepan of water to the boil and add a teaspoon of salt.

2. Add the carrots and cook for 2 minutes, then add the asparagus, fennel, and peas, cooking until all are tender, about 2-3 minutes longer. Drain and return to the pot, add the butter and herbs, toss through, and serve.

Coq au Vin Blanc

Ingredients

1.5kg chicken thighs

Sea salt and freshly ground black pepper

150g thick cut bacon, chopped

10 banana shallot onions

3 sprigs thyme

2 sprigs rosemary

3 tablespoons olive oil

300ml white wine

25g butter

350g button mushrooms, wiped and quartered

3 large cloves garlic, grated

200ml double cream

1 tablespoon chopped parsley

Serves 4

What you do

1 Preheat the oven to 220°C/Fan 200°C/Gas 7. Arrange the chicken pieces in a large casserole dish and scatter with the bacon, shallots, thyme, and rosemary. Season to taste with sea salt and freshly ground black pepper. Drizzle with 2 tablespoons of olive oil and roast for 20 minutes.

2 Add the wine to the casserole, cover and cook for another 20-25 minutes. Remove from the oven.

3 Heat the butter and remaining tablespoon of oil in a large frying pan over a medium heat. When the butter is foaming, add the mushrooms and garlic and fry for 3-5 minutes, pour in the cream and bubble for 3 minutes. Tip the creamy mushrooms and garlic into the casserole. Thicken the juice

with 1 heaped teaspoon of cornflour and 2 tablespoons of water (you may not need it all). Stir slowly until it resembles a double cream consistency. Finish with chopped parsley.

Pasta, Beans and Peas

Ingredients

300g penne, fresh or dried

150g French beans, trimmed and halved

150g peas

25g butter

1 teaspoon lemon zest

1 tablespoon lemon juice

A handful of fresh basil leaves

Sea salt and fresh black pepper to finish

Serves 4

What you do

1 Bring 3 litres of water, plus 1 teaspoon of salt, to the boil, add the penne and cook for 6 minutes. Add the beans and cook for 3 minutes, followed by the peas for 2 minutes.

2 Drain everything well and tip back into the hot pan.

3 Add the butter, lemon zest, juice, and tear in the basil. Stir through.

4 Season with a little sea salt and a few twists of black pepper.

Spring into Summer

Italian
Bundles
1 & 2

Pennoni Giardiniera
Penne with Spinach Fritters

Ingredients

For the spinach fritters

400g spinach, washed, large stalks removed

2 medium free-range eggs, beaten

¼ teaspoon freshly grated nutmeg

1 clove garlic, grated

125g soft breadcrumbs

60g Parmesan, grated

½ teaspoon sea salt

¼ teaspoon ground black pepper

3 tablespoons olive oil

Pasta sauce

4 tablespoons olive oil

2 cloves garlic, finely grated

1 small red chilli, deseeded and finely chopped

2 medium courgettes, trimmed and coarsely grated (don't use the central core of seeds)

50g Parmesan, grated

¼ teaspoon sea salt

⅛ teaspoon black pepper

Pasta

300g rigatoni – follow the cooking instructions on the packet and, when draining, save about 3 tablespoons of the water

Serves 4

What you do

1 **To make the spinach balls**
– Blanch the spinach leaves in a pan of salted, boiling water for 2 minutes, drain well and refresh in cold water, then drain again.

② Using your hands, squeeze out as much water from the blanched spinach leaves as possible, then finely chop them and pop into a bowl.

③ Stir in the beaten eggs, nutmeg, garlic purée, breadcrumbs and Parmesan. Season to taste with salt and freshly ground black pepper. Mix well until the mixture binds together, add more breadcrumbs or water if needed to bind the mixture.

④ Roll into walnut-sized balls and place on a baking tray.

⑤ Cover the base of a frying pan in a thin layer of olive oil and heat gently over a low to medium heat.

⑥ When the oil is hot, add the spinach balls in batches, about 6-8 at a time, depending on the size of your pan. Fry for about 5 minutes on each side until crisp and golden-brown all over. Remove with a slotted spoon onto kitchen paper to drain, then spoon onto a plate and

keep warm in a low temperature oven, about 60°C. Repeat the process with the remaining spinach balls.

⑦ **For the pasta sauce** – Heat the oil in a separate frying pan over a medium heat, add the garlic and chilli and fry for 2 minutes until softened but not coloured.

⑧ Stir in the courgettes and fry for about 4 minutes until they start to soften. Add the Parmesan and season, to taste, with salt and freshly ground black pepper. Mix until well combined, then stir in the reserved cooking water from the pasta and any liquid from the drained rigatoni.

⑨ To serve, divide the pasta and sauce equally among four warmed serving plates. Place the fried spinach balls on top and serve with a little extra grated Parmesan.

Milanese Chicken, Spaghetti with Tomato and Basil Velouté

Ingredients

Chicken

4 medium chicken breasts

1 tablespoon Dijon mustard

1 teaspoon paprika

1 teaspoon chopped rosemary

1 teaspoon grated lemon zest

1 flat teaspoon sea salt

$1/4$ teaspoon ground black pepper

100g plain flour

2 medium free-range eggs

200ml cold water

4 handfuls dried white or panko breadcrumbs

Sunflower or olive oil for shallow frying

Serves 4

What you do

1 I like to brine my chicken before cooking – see brine recipe (page 42) and use 2 x the recipe for this. Mix in a bowl and add the chicken breast fillets for 25 minutes.

2 Meanwhile, make the batter – place the mustard, paprika, rosemary, lemon zest, salt, pepper and flour into a mixing bowl. Mix together and make a well in the centre, break in the eggs, add the

water and beat together, then draw in the flour to produce a batter with the consistency of double cream. Set aside until the brining time is reached.

3 Drain the chicken and pat dry with kitchen paper. Cut each fillet in half, opening like a butterfly, and cut in two, keeping the shape of the fillet. Dip into the batter, coating completely, then coat in the breadcrumbs, gently pressing them into the fillet.

4 Heat the oil in a non-stick pan over a medium-low heat. When hot, add a couple of pieces of chicken, cooking on both sides until a rich golden colour. Drain on kitchen paper and keep warm in an oven at 70°C. Repeat until all the chicken is cooked. Serve with the spaghetti.

When we put our menus together, Olivia and I sit with a cuppa and discuss our favourite foods and just bring them together into yummy bundles. This is a real favourite at home and one of fussy eater Tom's (Olivia's man) as well; just the chicken though, no pasta and sauce for him!

Spaghetti with Tomato Velouté

Ingredients

Sauce

3 tablespoons olive oil

1 large onion, finely chopped

1 fat clove garlic, grated

1 teaspoon chopped thyme

100ml water

400g ripe tomatoes, chopped, fresh or tinned

2 tablespoons chopped oregano/1 teaspoon dried

200ml chicken or vegetable stock

Sea salt and black pepper

Pinch sugar

100ml double cream or crème fraîche

300g dried spaghetti

Serves 4

What you do

1 Heat the olive oil in a large pan, stir in the chopped onions and 100ml of water. Cook the onions really slowly until the water has evaporated and they have turned sticky and lightly golden. Stir in the garlic and thyme and cook for a minute.

2 Add the tomatoes, oregano, sea salt, pepper and sugar, then add the stock and cook until softened and thick in consistency, about 1 hour.

3 Meanwhile, bring a large saucepan of salted water to the boil, add the spaghetti and stir to

separate. Simmer until just cooked
(check the time on the packet
instructions). Blitz the sauce to
form a smooth sauce with a stick
blender, stir in the cream, taste and
adjust the seasoning as you prefer.

4 Drain the pasta really well and
add back into the saucepan, pour in
the sauce and stir over a low heat
for 5 minutes.

5 Serve with the chicken.

This sauce is so versatile – try
it with poached or grilled fish,
roasted chicken or vegetables,
or even poached eggs!

Veggie
Bundle 1

Spanish
Bundle

Chicken, Chorizo and White Beans with Manzanilla

Ingredients

4 chicken leg and thigh joints

1 tablespoon olive oil

Rub

1 flat teaspoon sea salt

½ teaspoon ground black pepper

1 rounded teaspoon garlic granules

1 heaped teaspoon smoked sweet paprika

Casserole

1 tablespoon olive oil

150g chorizo sausage, sliced

1 large onion, finely diced

1 large garlic clove, grated

1 bay leaf

1 sprig sage leaves

4 tablespoons Manzanilla sherry

1 x 400g tin chopped tomatoes

300ml chicken stock

1 tablespoon sundried tomato paste

½ teaspoon sugar

1 x 420g butter or cannelini beans, drained and rinsed

Serves 4

What you do

1 Wipe the chicken joints with kitchen paper. Rub all over with the olive oil.

2 Make the rub by mixing all the ingredients together and sprinkle liberally all over the chicken.

3 To make the casserole, heat the oil in a heavy-based pan or dish that has a lid. Add the chicken joints and brown all over, remove and pop on a plate.

4 Add the chorizo to the pan and cook to release the oil, stir in the onions, add 4 tablespoons of water and cover with a lid. Cook until soft and turning lightly golden. Add the garlic, bay, sage, and sherry, stir through, and then add the tomatoes, stock, sundried tomato paste, and sugar.

5 Bring to the boil, add the chicken joints back in and reduce the temperature to a gentle simmer. Stir in the beans and cook for 1 hour.

Echoes of trips to sunny Spain are captured in this delicious one-pot dish. Many people have been missing their annual holidays and this is a simple recipe that can recreate those intense flavours from slow-cooked Spanish cuisine.

Rice with Saffron, Raisins and Parsley

Ingredients

80g raisins

3 cloves garlic, peeled and grated

1 small onion, peeled and sliced thinly

2 tablespoons olive oil

200g long grain rice

400ml cold water/vegetable stock

1 teaspoon saffron threads, soaked in 1 tablespoon hot water from a boiled kettle

Sea salt and freshly ground black pepper

4 tablespoons chopped parsley

Serves 4

What you do

1 Pop the raisins into a bowl, cover with hot water and set aside.

2 Heat a non-stick frying pan over a medium heat, add the olive oil, then the onion and stir through.

3 Cook until softened and lightly golden. Stir in the garlic, cook for 1 minute, then add the rice and stir through.

4 Add the soaked raisins, the saffron with the liquid, 1 teaspoon of sea salt and 6 twists of black pepper.

5 Pour in the water/stock, stir through and bring to the boil. Reduce the heat to a slow simmer, cover and leave to cook for 8 minutes without stirring. Remove

the lid and check if the rice is cooked through; if it needs a little longer, stir through and replace the lid for a couple of minutes.

6 To finish, stir in the chopped parsley and check the taste, seasoning more if required.

This Spanish bundle really captures the essence of this cuisine and was a real treat for all those missing their holidays.

Ratatouille Provençal Bake with Orzo

Ingredients

6 tablespoons olive oil

2 yellow onions, sliced

4 cloves garlic, roughly chopped

4-5 medium tomatoes, sliced

4 small to medium courgettes, sliced

2 medium aubergines, trimmed and sliced

1 medium yellow pepper, sliced

1 medium green pepper, sliced

1 teaspoon dried thyme

¼ teaspoon dried dill

2 tablespoons fresh oregano leaves (or 1 teaspoon dried)

1 tablespoon sundried tomato paste

2 tablespoons fresh basil leaves, chopped (or 1 teaspoon dried)

Pasta base

200g orzo

400ml passata

1 teaspoon sugar

½ teaspoon vegetable bouillon powder

A handful of shredded basil leaves

Sea salt and black pepper

200g cream cheese

Serves 4

What you do

1 Preheat oven to 200°C/Fan 180°C/Gas 6.

2 Take 2 frying pans, add 2 tablespoons of oil to each and heat over a medium temperature. Add the sliced onions and peppers to one

pan and stir through; add the sliced courgette to the other. Season both with sea salt, pepper and a little sugar and stir through. Cook until the onions and peppers are really soft and stir in a little of the herbs.

③ Cook the courgettes until they are just beginning to soften and season with a little of the herbs, as above.

④ Once the onions and peppers are soft, remove with a slotted spoon and set on a large plate or baking sheet. Remove the courgettes and set aside with the onions and peppers.

⑤ Now slice the aubergine and fry in both pans, adding a little more olive oil, salt, pepper and sugar. When they just start to soften, add the remaining herbs and stir through. Remove from the heat and spoon onto the plate/baking sheet. Slice the tomatoes; if large, cut in half before slicing. Set aside.

⑥ Cook the orzo in salted water according to the instructions on the packet. Drain. Heat the passata in a pan, add the cooked orzo, vegetable powder, sugar, half of the basil, salt and pepper to taste. Tip into the base of a nice casserole or gratin dish and dot with the cream cheese.

⑦ Top with the onions and peppers first, followed by overlapping alternate slices of courgette, aubergine and tomato – you may have to do 2 layers if your dish is small. Brush with oil from the pan and the tomato paste.

⑧ Cover tightly with foil and bake for about an hour, or until the veggies are bubbling and the aubergine is soft.

⑨ Remove from the oven, sprinkle with the remaining fresh basil and serve immediately. It is excellent as a side dish, or served with toasted slices of French bread.

Greek
Bundles

Smoked Stuffed Aubergines

Ingredients

2 large aubergines

3 tablespoons olive oil

1 medium onion, finely chopped

2 garlic cloves, finely chopped, then pasted

$\frac{1}{2}$ teaspoon dried thyme

$\frac{1}{2}$ teaspoon dried oregano

$\frac{1}{2}$ teaspoon dried red chilli flakes (optional)

2 tomatoes, skinned and roughly chopped, or 6 tablespoons tinned chopped tomatoes

25g white breadcrumbs (ciabatta or focaccia are good)

25g Parmesan or Pecorino, or an alternative vegetarian hard cheese, freshly grated

$\frac{1}{2}$ unwaxed lemon, grated zest only

A handful fresh oregano and parsley leaves, shredded

Sea salt and freshly ground black pepper

Serves 4

What you do

1 Preheat oven to 200°C/Fan 180°C/Gas 6 or set your BBQ for indirect heat 200°C and soak two handfuls of woodchips for smoking. Cut the aubergines in half lengthways, and, leaving a border of around 5mm/$\frac{1}{4}$in, cut out the flesh.

2 Dice the flesh and set aside. Brush the inside of the aubergines with olive oil and season with salt. Place in a baking tin and cover with

foil. Bake for 20 minutes in the oven or on the BBQ.

3 Heat 2 tablespoons of the olive oil in a pan. Add the onion and fry gently over a medium heat for 10 minutes, or until softened.

4 Increase the heat, add the garlic and aubergine flesh and stir until the aubergine has lightly browned. Add the herbs, chilli flakes, if using, and the tomatoes and season with salt and pepper. Stir to combine, reduce the heat and cover.

5 Simmer for 10 minutes, remove the lid and continue to cook until any liquid has evaporated.

6 Spoon the mixture into the aubergine halves. Mix the breadcrumbs with the cheese, lemon zest, oregano and parsley leaves and season with a little salt and pepper. Sprinkle this over the stuffed aubergines and drizzle with more olive oil.

7 Bake the aubergines, uncovered, for 25-30 minutes, or until the filling is hot through and the top has lightly browned. If you are cooking them on the BBQ, place over indirect heat, add half the soaked woodchips to each charcoal pile and close the lid. Smoke for about 20-25 minutes.

8 To serve, I like these with a dollop of Greek-style yoghurt with some chopped mint.

We use the BBQ and soaked woodchips to smoke the aubergines, however, if you want to keep the cooking indoors, replace the sea salt with smoked sea salt and use a teaspoon of smoked paprika in your filling.

Skordalia

Ingredients

300g potatoes

4 large garlic cloves, grated

90g whole blanched almonds

Sea salt

60ml olive oil

60ml water

2 tablespoons lemon juice

1 tablespoon white wine vinegar

Serves 4

What you do

1 Boil the potatoes in their skins or wrap them in foil and cook on the BBQ until soft through – about 45 minutes to 1 hour. Once the potatoes are soft through, remove from the pan/BBQ and cool slightly. Peel away the skins, cut into large chunks and pass through a potato ricer directly into a mixing bowl. Alternatively, use a potato masher and make sure there are no lumps.

2 In a food processor, combine the garlic, almonds, olive oil and whiz into a paste. Mix this into the potatoes until incorporated, then mix in 1 flat dessertspoon of sea salt, the water, lemon juice and vinegar and season with pepper to taste. Serve at room temperature.

Greek Meatballs with Feta

Ingredients

Meatballs

400g lamb mince

200g lean beef mince

1 small red onion, finely chopped

3 cloves garlic, crushed

75g Greek yoghurt, plus extra to serve

75g soft breadcrumbs

1 tbsp dried oregano

1 teaspoon ground black pepper

2 teaspoons sea salt

4 tablespoons olive oil

Sauce

1 red onion, finely chopped

2½ teaspoons ground cinnamon

1½ teaspoons dried chilli flakes

2 tablespoons runny honey

2 tablespoons fresh (or 1 dessertspoon dried) oregano, chopped

Sea salt and black pepper to taste

400g tinned chopped tomatoes

1 tablespoon sundried tomato paste

600g passata

200ml red wine

To Finish

200g feta

A handful flat-leaf parsley, chopped, to serve

25g pine nuts, toasted

Bread, couscous, or orzo to serve

Serves 4

What you do

1 Put all the ingredients for the meatballs into a bowl and mash together with 1 teaspoon of ground black pepper and 2 teaspoons of sea salt. Roll into 18 fat meatballs and chill for 30 minutes.

2 Heat the oven to 170°C/Fan 150°C/Gas 3. Put the olive oil in a frying pan and then, in batches, brown the meatballs well on all sides. Scoop out and drain on kitchen paper.

3 Pour off any oil, add the chopped onions and cook until soft (add a little water here to steam fry and speed up the process). Stir in the cinnamon, chilli flakes, honey, salt, pepper and oregano and cook for 1 minute.

4 Add the wine and stir through, cook for 30 seconds, then add the chopped tomatoes, sundried tomato paste and passata and bring to the boil, scraping up all the meaty bits as you do. Transfer to a deep baking dish or oven tray. Sit the meatballs in the sauce, then cover the whole dish with foil. Bake for 1 hour and 30 minutes.

5 Turn the heat up to 220°C/Fan 200°C/Gas 7. Remove the foil and break over the feta in chunks, then put back in the oven for 15 minutes. When it is ready, scatter with parsley, sprinkle with pine nuts and dollop with a little Greek yoghurt, should you wish. Serve with bread, couscous, or orzo.

Little Greek Roast Potatoes

Ingredients

1.5kg starchy potatoes

300ml chicken stock

100ml olive oil

75ml lemon juice

4 large garlic cloves, grated

1 tablespoon dried oregano

1 rounded teaspoon sea salt

Serves 4

What you do

1 Preheat the oven to 180°C/Fan 160°C/Gas 4.

2 Peel the potatoes and cut into thick wedges.

3 Place in a roasting pan with all the other ingredients and toss together. Cover with foil and bake in the oven for 30 minutes.

4 To crisp the potatoes, remove the foil and turn up the heat to 200°C/Fan 180°C/Gas 6 and roast for a further 25 minutes, turning once or twice, until potatoes are golden and a bit crispy.

Greek Salad Salsa

Ingredients

½ small red onion, sliced thinly

1 tablespoon white wine vinegar

1 medium cucumber, peeled, quartered, and deseeded

4 medium-large ripe tomatoes

100g feta cheese, drained

8 black Kalamata olives

¼ teaspoon sugar

4 tablespoons Greek olive oil

¼ teaspoon fresh ground black pepper

1 teaspoon fresh chopped oregano or ½ teaspoon dried oregano

Serves 4

What you do

1 Mix the red onion slices with the vinegar and set aside to cure.

2 Cut the cucumber, tomato and feta into small dice and place in a bowl. Quarter the olives and stir into the bowl.

3 Add the sugar, olive oil, black pepper and herbs to the onions and vinegar, mix together, pour over the salad and serve.

A mini version of the usual Greek salad, packed full of flavour and perfect with the dishes above.

Chinese Bundles

Lemon Chicken

Ingredients

1.5kg chicken breast fillets, each cut in half, keeping the shape of the fillets

Marinade

2 tablespoons dry sherry

2 tablespoons light soy sauce

1 large clove garlic, grated

1 heaped teaspoon finely chopped ginger

1½ flat teaspoon sea salt

Coating

100g plain flour

2 large eggs, beaten

1 garlic clove, grated

1 teaspoon sea salt

1 tablespoon light soy sauce

100ml cold water

4 large handfuls panko

breadcrumbs

Sunflower oil for frying

Sauce

1 tablespoon sunflower oil

½ lemon, thinly sliced (save the rest for the zest and juice below)

300ml good flavoured chicken stock

1 teaspoon grated lemon zest

60-100ml lemon juice, depending on how sharp you like your sauce

50g sugar

1 tablespoon cornflour

Sea salt to taste

1 lemon, thinly sliced

2 spring onions, chopped

1 dessertspoon toasted sesame seeds to finish

Serves 4

What you do

1 Prepare the chicken into half fillets, cutting through each of them to create two halves. Mix the sherry, soy, garlic, ginger, and sea salt in a large bowl. Add the chicken, coat in the mixture, cover and chill for a couple of hours or even overnight.

2 When ready to cook, prepare the coating batter by mixing the flour, eggs, garlic, salt, soy sauce and 100ml cold water, whisking to form a smooth paste.

3 Heat a large non-stick pan, add a layer of sunflower oil and heat.

4 Dip the marinated chicken into the batter, press into the panko breadcrumbs and then into the hot pan. Cook in batches and fry slowly until a rich golden colour and cooked through, about 7 minutes each side. Remove and keep warm in the oven at 70°C.

5 Continue to cook the remaining chicken.

6 **To make the sauce –** Heat the oil in a frying pan, add the lemon slices and fry until caramelized, remove and set aside.

7 Pour the chicken stock into a saucepan and place over a medium-high heat until hot. Add the lemon zest, juice, and sugar. Dissolve the cornflour in a little water and whisk into the stock. Bring to the boil, stirring all the time, reduce the heat once slightly thickened. Pour over the chicken and sprinkle with the lemon slices, chopped spring onion and toasted sesame seeds.

I have recently revisited some classic dishes and personalised them to suit our palate and we really enjoyed the results, as did our customers.

Cucumber Salad

Ingredients

1 large cucumber, peeled

3 large cloves garlic, grated

1 tablespoon rice wine vinegar

1 tablespoon light soy sauce

1 teaspoon sugar

½ teaspoon sea salt

1 teaspoon toasted sesame oil

1-2 teaspoons chilli oil

Serves 4

What you do

1 Dry the cucumber with a paper towel and place on a large chopping board. Cover with a sheet of cling film and lightly bash with a rolling pin – this will soften it a little.

2 Remove the cling film and cut into good bite-sized pieces, place in a bowl and stir in the garlic. If you are not serving the salad immediately, cover and pop in the fridge.

3 To make the dressing, mix the vinegar, soy sauce, sugar, salt, and sesame oil in a small bowl and mix well. Cover and set aside.

4 When you are ready to serve, pour the dressing mixture over the cucumber and mix well. (Do not add the sauce beforehand, as it will cause the cucumber to lose water and the sauce will be diluted.) To give the salad an extra kick, you can drizzle some chilli oil or sprinkle with a little flaked chilli.

A deliciously refreshing surprise!

Special Fried Rice

Ingredients

2 large eggs, beaten and cooked into an omelette, rolled up and sliced

1 tablespoon vegetable oil

1 small onion, finely sliced

50g chopped pancetta or bacon

1 fat clove garlic, pasted with sea salt

1 spring onion, chopped

50g frozen peas

500g cooked rice

½ teaspoon bouillon powder

A sprinkle of 5-spice powder, salt, and white pepper to taste

Serves 4

What you do

1 Heat the oil in a wok, add the onion and pancetta, cooking until soft, then add the garlic, spring onion and peas, cooking for 2 minutes.

2 Stir in the rice, bouillon and egg, sprinkle with 5-spice powder, season to taste, cover and leave over a low heat to ensure the rice is cooked through.

3 Add a little water if needed – this will help steam the rice through without sticking to the pan.

4 Add some chopped coriander to finish if you wish.

Barbecued Char Sui Pork with Sticky Sauce

Ingredients

1.5kg pork tenderloin, fully trimmed of sinew

Marinade/Sauce

50g soft brown sugar

1 teaspoon 5-spice powder

¼ teaspoon white pepper

½ teaspoon sesame oil

1 tablespoon Shaoxing rice wine

60ml maltose or runny honey

60ml hoisin sauce

2 tablespoons light soy sauce

3 cloves garlic, grated

1 tablespoon hot water

Serves 4

What you do

1 Mix the ingredients for the marinade/sauce in a bowl.

2 Use three-quarters of the mixture to spread all over the pork, wrap and leave to marinade in the fridge overnight.

3 When you are ready to cook the next day, remove the pork from the fridge half an hour before cooking.

4 Pour the remaining marinade/sauce into a small saucepan, bring to the boil and simmer for 3 minutes (it will thicken slightly).

Leave to cool, cover, and set aside.

⑤ Set your oven to 220°C/Fan 200°C/Gas 7, or your BBQ to 220°C.

⑥ Line a baking sheet or, if using the BBQ, a convection tray with baking parchment.

⑦ Roast for 25 minutes, basting with the reserved sticky marinade twice throughout the cooking time, which will build up a sticky glaze.

⑧ I usually test the pork with a temperature probe – it should be 72°C at the centre. The temperature will climb slightly as the pork rests.

⑨ Loosely cover with foil and rest for 10-15 minutes before serving.

⑩ Slice and spoon any remaining juices over the top.

Asian Shredded Noodle Salad with Mango Relish

Ingredients

200g brown rice noodles or pad Thai-style noodles

300g mixed shredded vegetables, such as carrots, cabbage, radish, sweet pepper, courgette

3 spring onions, trimmed and thinly sliced

12 stems and leaves of coriander, chopped

1 teaspoon deseeded chilli, finely chopped

2 tablespoons salted peanuts, finely chopped (optional)

Relish

200g fresh mango, peeled and diced

1-2 teaspoons sugar or honey

½ teaspoon sea salt

1 small clove garlic, grated

1 level teaspoon finely chopped ginger

6 tablespoons lime juice

¼ teaspoon deseeded chilli, chopped

4 stems and leaves of coriander, chopped

Serves 4

What you do

1 Cook the noodles according to the instructions on the packet, drain and cool under running water. Shake off the excess water and tip into a large bowl. Add the vegetables, spring onions, coriander and chilli and mix.

2 Keep covered in the fridge until you are ready to serve.

3 Make the relish by adding everything together in a mixing bowl and keep covered in the fridge until needed.

4 When you are ready to serve, remove both the noodle salad and relish from the fridge and toss together. Finish with the peanuts, if using, and serve with the pork.

Spring Onion and Sesame Flat Bread

Ingredients

350g strong white bread flour, plus extra to dust

1½ teaspoon fast-action yeast

1 teaspoon sugar

1 teaspoon sea salt

100ml warm water

5 tablespoons natural yoghurt

2 tablespoons melted butter, plus extra to brush

Cooking and finishing

Sunflower oil for cooking

3 tablespoons spring onion, finely chopped

1 tablespoon sesame seeds

Serves 4

What you do

1 Put the flour and yeast into a large mixing bowl and stir to combine, then mix in the sugar and salt. Make a well in the centre and pour in the water, yoghurt and melted butter, mix both together then combine with the flour to form a soft dough.

2 Tip out on a lightly floured surface and knead for about 5 minutes until smooth and a little less sticky, then put in a large, lightly oiled bowl and turn to coat. Cover and leave in a draught-free place (the airing cupboard, or an unlit oven) until it has doubled in size – roughly 60-90 minutes.

Tip the dough back out onto the lightly floured surface and knock the air out, then divide into 8 balls (or 6 if you have a particularly large frying pan).

③ Heat a non-stick frying pan over a high heat for 5 minutes and put the oven on low. Flatten one of the balls and roll it into a flat circle, sprinkle with some chopped spring onion and sesame seeds and roll over again so they stick. Brush the hot pan with sunflower oil and pop the flatbread into the pan. When it starts to bubble, lift it up on a spatula, re-oil the pan and cook the other side of the bread until browned in patches. Turn it back over and cook until there are no doughy bits remaining. Repeat until all the breads are cooked and keep them stacked in the low-temperature oven to keep warm.

④ To make ahead and store, pile the breads on top of each other and seal in foil. Reheat at 160°C/Fan 140°C/Gas 3 for 10 minutes, remove the foil for 2 minutes and serve.

Flat breads don't appear in Chinese cooking, but we thought the texture and flavours were just brilliant with the pork and the relish. They go well with lots of dishes, so give them a try.

Asian Bundle
& Veggie
Bundle 2

Asian Poached Chicken

Ingredients

Poaching

4 free-range chicken breasts

6 coriander stems

1 teaspoon black peppercorns

3 spring onions, washed and trimmed

1 tablespoon sea salt

2 small red chillies

Salad

250g French beans, trimmed

200g greens e.g. spinach, bok choy, kale

100g rice noodles, soaked in cold water for 20 minutes

Dressing

3 tablespoons light soy sauce

2 tablespoons rice wine or white wine vinegar

3 tablespoons mirrin

1 teaspoon sesame oil

3 fat cloves garlic, finely grated

1 tablespoon ginger, finely chopped

1 tablespoon sesame seeds, toasted

Serves 4

What you do

1 Place the coriander, peppercorns, spring onions, sea salt and chillies in a pan three-quarters full of water and bring to the boil. Add the chicken and poach for 10 minutes, then switch off the heat

and leave the chicken in the broth for 20 minutes.

② Meanwhile, make the salad. Blanch the beans in a pan of salted water for 4-5 minutes – they should be bright in colour and still a little crisp. Add the leafy greens and rice noodles for 2 minutes then drain well.

③ To make the dressing, heat the soy, vinegar, mirrin and sesame oil in a small saucepan and then add the garlic and ginger.

④ To serve, remove the chicken, drain, and slice on an angle.

⑤ Make a bed of the greens and noodles on each plate, top with the chicken and pour the dressing over the top, finishing with the sesame seeds.

This recipe is inspired by Aussie chef and food writer Bill Granger. Olivia and I met him at the Abergavenny Food Festival years ago and he was a delight! We love his fresh approach to food and the Asian influences he brings to his dishes.

Prawn and Sesame Toasts

Ingredients

Topping

300g peeled prawns, drained

1 medium egg white

1 fat clove garlic, grated

1 teaspoon chopped ginger

2 teaspoons light soy sauce

1 tablespoon cornflour

½ teaspoon sea salt

2 spring onions, trimmed and finely chopped

The rest

4 slices medium cut white bread, crusts trimmed

2 beaten eggs with a little water

4 tablespoons sesame seeds

Sunflower oil for deep-frying

Serves 4

What you do

1 Put all the ingredients for the topping in a food processor and blend to a paste. Spread the paste on 1 side of the bread and press down, forming a nice even spread. Cut each slice into 2 triangles.

2 Dip the prawn side into the egg then press into the sesame seeds.

3 Heat 4 inches of oil in a pan or wok (I use a frying pan) until hot but not smoking. Place your toasts into the oil and fry for 30 to 50 seconds each side until golden. Drain well on kitchen paper before serving.

Courgette, Olive and Feta Filo Tart

Ingredients

3 tablespoons olive oil

8 sheets filo pastry

75g focaccia breadcrumbs

300g courgettes, coarsely grated

100g cooked soft onions

60g green olives, halved

1 tablespoon mixed herbs e.g. parsley, chives, dill, or basil

6 large eggs

2 lemons, zest only

200ml crème fraiche

250g feta cheese, crumbled

Serves 4

What you do

1 Preheat the oven to 180°C/ Fan 160°C/Gas 4 and pop a baking sheet inside to heat up. Use a little of the oil to lightly grease an 18 x 25cm/3cm deep tart tin. Line the tin with baking parchment, as this will help you lift the tart out later.

2 Unfold the filo pastry, keeping it covered with a damp tea towel as you work to prevent it from drying out. Taking 1 sheet at a time, brush each piece well with oil and line your tart tin with it, leaving a little pastry hanging over the edges. Sprinkle a thin layer of breadcrumbs between each layer of pastry as you go, as this will help to keep the pastry crisp.

3 When you get to the final layer, brush with a little extra oil and scrunch the edges together and fold inwards slightly to create a border.

4 Toss the courgettes with seasoning and the remaining oil and tip onto a baking tray. Place the pastry case on the top shelf of the oven with the courgettes on the shelf below and cook for 10 minutes.

5 Remove the courgettes from the oven. Brush the tart with a little beaten egg and bake for a further 5 minutes until the pastry is golden brown and crunchy.

6 Whisk the remaining eggs with the lemon zest, crème fraîche and seasoning. Lay half the courgette, onion and olives and herbs in the bottom of the pastry case and add half the feta. Pour over the egg mixture and top with the remaining courgettes, onion, olives, herbs and feta.

7 Bake for 40 minutes until the filling has set. Remove from the oven and leave to cool.

Tomato Salad with Herbes de Provence

Ingredients

6 medium ripe tomatoes – plum, rose or heritage are excellent

400g cherry tomatoes on the vine

6 tablespoons olive oil

Topping

2 teaspoons sea salt

1½ teaspoon sugar

½ teaspoon garlic granules

1 dessertspoon Herbes de Provence

1 teaspoon Dijon mustard

Fresh ground black pepper

12 basil leaves to finish

Serves 4

What you do

1 Slice the medium tomatoes and lay them out on a large plate. Sprinkle with 1 teaspoon of sea salt and set aside for 1 hour.

2 Meanwhile, cut the cherry tomatoes around the middle and lay them on an oven tray lined with baking parchment. Brush with some of the olive oil.

3 Mix the remaining salt, sugar, garlic granules and dried herbs and sprinkle liberally over the tomatoes.

4 Cook in a preheated oven at 150°C/Fan 130°C/Gas 2 for 1 hour, when they should be a little shrivelled and brown at the edges.

⑤ Drain the juices from the sliced tomatoes into a mixing bowl and whisk in the Dijon mustard and remaining olive oil, plus any roasting juices from the cherry tomatoes.

⑥ Arrange the tomato slices on a serving plate, top with the roasted tomatoes, spoon over the dressing and finish with a few twists of freshly ground black pepper and torn basil.

Summer into Autumn

BBQ
Bundle
& Italian
Bundle 3

Hot Smoked Barbecued Beef with Chilli Sauce

Ingredients

1.5kg piece beef knuckle or similar for slow cook (chuck, blade, brisket, or skirt)

1 quantity of brine – see page 120

2 tablespoons olive oil

3 wood chunks for smoking e.g. hickory, pecan or oak

Flavourings

1 small red chilli, split

2 cloves garlic, smashed

1 teaspoon coriander seeds

1 shallot, sliced

Rub

1 teaspoon each of cumin and fennel seeds, black peppercorns, sugar, cocoa powder

2 teaspoons each of coriander seeds, garlic granules, dried oregano, chipotle, ancho chilli flakes, smoked paprika

Sauce

4 tablespoons olive oil

1 medium onion, peeled and finely chopped

2 large cloves garlic, peeled and grated

400g tinned chopped tomatoes

300ml beef or chicken stock

1 tablespoon sundried tomato paste

1 teaspoon instant coffee or shot of espresso

Sea salt and black pepper

Serves 4

What you do

1 First, prepare the beef for the BBQ, doing it the same way if cooking in the oven. Prepare the brine, add the flavourings and mix well, add the chunk of beef, cover, and pop in the fridge for 1 hour.

2 Next, make the rub by taking a small frying pan, and placing it over a medium heat. Add all the whole spices – cumin, fennel, black pepper, and coriander seeds. Roast until fragrant, stirring through so they roast evenly.

3 Remove from the heat and tip into a spice/coffee grinder, pulse to form a fine powder and mix with the rest of the rub ingredients.

4 Make the sauce by heating the oil in a pan, add the onion, stir through, and cook over a medium heat adding 4 tablespoons of water to help steam cook the onion. Once soft and deliciously golden, add the garlic and cook for a couple of minutes., then half of the spice mix, cook for 1 minute. Pour in the tomatoes, stock, tomato paste and coffee, bring to the boil, then reduce to a slow simmer and cook until thickened nicely, approximately 45 minutes. Taste and season with salt and pepper.

5 When the hour is up, remove the beef from the brine, pat dry with kitchen paper. Apply the oil and rub all over, followed by the remaining spice mix, and pat all over.

6 Set your BBQ smoker between 110-110°C or your oven to 135°C/ Fan 110°C/Gas 1.

7 Add 3 soaked wood chunks to the BBQ coals and place the prepared beef in a foil tray with 200ml of water and smoke/slow cook for 2½ -3 hours.

8 If roasting in an oven, place the beef in a roasting tin with 200ml of water and roast for the same time. Baste at half hour intervals using both methods. Add the sauce to the beef tray after 2 hours of cooking and stir around so it mixes with the juices in the tin.

9 Once the beef is cooked, rest for 15-20 minutes before carving.

Such a full-bodied dish, it earned us some rave reviews from our customers. If you are not using a smoker, use smoked sea salt in place of regular salt and add double the amount of smoked paprika to the rub.

Brazilian Slaw

Ingredients

400g white or green cabbage, sliced thinly

¼ red onion, thinly sliced and soaked in 1 tablespoon wine or cider vinegar for 20 minutes

½ teaspoon sea salt

250-300g fresh pineapple, peeled, cored, and chopped into 4cm pieces

3 spring onions, trimmed and sliced

Dressing

1 tablespoon sunflower oil

4 tablespoons lime juice

2 teaspoons honey

½ teaspoon sea salt

4 twists ground black pepper

1 tablespoon chopped coriander (optional)

1 lime, cut into wedges, to serve

Serves 4

What you do

1 Put the sliced cabbage in a bowl, drain the onion and mix in.

2 Sprinkle in the salt and mix well. Add the pineapple pieces, juice and the sliced spring onions and toss together.

3 Make the dressing by mixing everything together, add this 20 minutes before serving and garnish with the lime wedges.

Lasagne al Forno

Ingredients

Ragu Sauce

3 tablespoons olive oil

250g onion, finely diced

1 large carrot, peeled and finely diced

1 large stick celery, peeled, trimmed, and finely chopped

2 fat cloves of garlic, peeled and grated

6 stems thyme (1 level teaspoon of dried will also do)

1 bay leaf

1 heaped teaspoon dried oregano

500g lean minced beef

200ml white wine

500ml tinned tomatoes, whizzed up

300ml chicken stock

½ teaspoon of sugar

Parmesan rind, if you have it (optional)

2 heaped tablespoons sundried tomato paste

Béchamel Sauce

50g butter

50g plain flour

450ml full-fat milk

150ml double cream or crème fraîche

1 teaspoon vegetable bouillon powder (Swiss Marigold)

Sea salt to taste and ¼ teaspoon each of white pepper and freshly grated nutmeg

Other Bits

1 pack buffalo mozzarella – approximately 125g

200g full-fat cream cheese

100g grated Parmesan

9 cooked lasagne sheets (use hand-

made, fresh packet, or dried lasagne sheets, following the instructions on the packet to cook them)

Serves 4

What you do

1 Preheat the oven to 190°C/Fan 170°C/Gas 5.

2 To make the ragu, spread the onion, carrot and celery in a parchment-lined roasting tin. Season lightly with salt and pepper and drizzle over 2 tablespoons of olive oil, mix well and spread out again. Cover with foil and bake for 35 minutes, stirring halfway through the cooking time.

3 Remove the veggies from the oven and scrape into a preheated sauté pan. Add the remaining olive oil, garlic and herbs and cook over a medium heat until soft and slightly sticky – this bit is important for the flavour.

4 Once the veggies start to colour a little, crumble in the beef mince and stir through so all the rawness is cooked out. Pour in the wine, then the tomatoes, stock, Parmesan rind (if using) and sundried tomato paste, stir through and bring to the boil. Turn the heat down so that the pan is barely simmering, cover and cook for 2 hours. Remove the lid and stir occasionally. To finish, taste and adjust with salt, pepper and a ½ teaspoon of sugar, or more if needed. Set aside to cool whilst you make the béchamel sauce.

5 To make the béchamel sauce, melt the butter in a pan over a medium heat. Stir in the flour and cook for 1 minute. Remove from the heat and gradually whisk in the milk and cream or crème fraiche. Return to the heat and bring to the boil, stirring constantly.

6 Reduce the heat slightly and simmer for 5 minutes, stirring until thickened, then add the vegetable bouillon, white pepper, sea salt and nutmeg. Taste and adjust with more seasoning if required. Stir in 2 tablespoons of the grated Parmesan, season and set aside.

7 Drain the mozzarella and shred into thin strips.

8 **To assemble the lasagne –** Use a nice deepish gratin dish, a small roasting tin or square/rectangular foil container. Spoon one-third of the ragu into the base and top with 3 sheets of cooked lasagne.

9 Repeat again but add a layer of mozzarella and one-third of the béchamel sauce on top of the ragu before the pasta sheets.

10 On the final layer, add the ragu and dot the cream cheese over the top before adding the final layer of pasta.

11 Finish with the remaining béchamel and remaining grated Parmesan to create a delicious crust.

12 Place on a baking sheet and bake for 45 minutes until bubbling and golden. Leave it to stand for 10 minutes before serving, as it will cut better.

This is not a dish to rush, but to cherish! The meat ragu can also be used for a bolognese-style spaghetti dish, so make double and freeze half for later.

Focaccia with Wild Garlic Pesto

Ingredients

Dough

500g bread flour

350g warm water

15g sea salt

7g easy bake yeast

85g olive oil

Wild Garlic Pesto

150g wild garlic, or a mix of basil and parsley

50g finely grated Parmesan

1 clove garlic, finely chopped

1 teaspoon lemon zest

50g pine nuts or pistachio nuts

150ml rapeseed oil or olive oil

Serves 4

What you do

1 Put the flour into a large bowl, make a well in the centre and add the water, sea salt, yeast and olive oil. Whisk and then combine everything with your hand to give a soft stretchy dough. Note: Hold back some of the water as you may need less or a little more depending on the flour. That is a rule for all breads.

2 Leave the dough for 5 minutes. Oil your work surface and hands and, using a dough scraper, remove the dough onto the surface. Pick it up with oiled hands and throw it forward onto your surface, keeping hold of one end so it extends and elongates on contact with the surface. Fold back towards you and repeat this process for 5 minutes until the dough is smooth and firmer. Have patience, you may need to use your dough scraper to help initially. Place on an oiled sheet and cover with cling film.

3 Let the dough rest for about an hour, or until doubled in size.

4 **To make the pesto –** Rinse and roughly chop the wild garlic leaves or the basil and parsley.

5 Blitz the wild garlic leaves, Parmesan, garlic, lemon zest and pine/pistachio nuts to a rough paste in a food processor. Season with ¼ teaspoon sea salt and then, with the motor running, add the oil.

6 Taste, season and add a few squeezes of lemon juice to balance. You will not need all of this for the bread, so serve some on the side at the table.

7 Tip the rested dough onto an oiled surface and gently flatten it slightly. Fold one end to the middle and the other end over the top – like making puff pastry. Seal the ends, turn so one end is nearest to you and press it out using your fingertips, starting at the centre and making dimples along the rectangle. Place back on the oiled baking sheet, cover and leave for another 30 minutes.

8 Repeat the folding and pressing out, place back on the baking sheet again and use your fingers to create an even dimpled finish on the dough. Spread the wild garlic pesto over the surface. Cover and rest for 30 minutes until increased in size again.

9 Bake in a preheated oven at 220°C/Fan 200°C/Gas 7 for 20-25 minutes. Rotate the bread 180° after the first 10 minutes to ensure even baking. Remove from the oven and then using a palette knife, immediately remove the focaccia onto a cooling rack. Cool for at least 20 minutes before cutting into slices.

Southern
Bundles

Southern Fried Chicken

Ingredients

6 free-range chicken thighs

6 free-range chicken legs

Flavour blend

1 dessertspoon dried thyme

1 dessertspoon dried basil

1 rounded teaspoon dried oregano

1 tablespoon celery salt

1 tablespoon dried mustard powder

4 tablespoons smoked paprika

2 tablespoons garlic granules

1 tablespoon ground ginger

½ teaspoon sugar

Brine/marinade

300ml full-fat milk

200ml yoghurt

2 egg whites

1 rounded teaspoon sea salt

2 dried bay leaves

1 heaped teaspoon soft brown sugar

1 tablespoon ground white pepper

300ml buttermilk

2 eggs, beaten

Frying

250g plain flour

1 tablespoon cornflour

1 teaspoon baking soda

1 dessertspoon sea salt

Serves 4

What you do

1 Blend together all the ingredients in the flavour blend list. Pat the chicken joints dry with kitchen paper and sprinkle with ½ the flavour, mixing on both sides.

2 Take a large mixing bowl, add the brine/marinade ingredients and beat together. Add the chicken joints and push under the liquid. Cover and keep in the fridge overnight.

3 When you are ready to cook, remove the bowl of chicken from the fridge and leave to climatise for 40 minutes.

4 Mix the remaining flavour blend with the flour, cornflour, baking soda and sea salt and mix everything together. Remove the chicken joints one at a time from the marinade and push into the seasoned flour, coating each really well.

5 Use a deep-frying pan or skillet for cooking the chicken. Fill two-thirds with sunflower oil and heat to 176°C/350°F. Cook the chicken in batches; it should take approximately 18 minutes and be golden and crisp.

6 Remove with tongs to a warm baking sheet and pop in a warmed oven at 150°C/Fan 130°C/Gas 2. Repeat to cook the remaining chicken.

This dish was a marathon when we made 86 portions of it for our orders. However, take heart and get excited as you prepare this king of the South dish. Just follow the recipe and you will have finger-licking great chicken!

Mac 'n' Cheese

Ingredients

100g extra mature cheddar cheese, grated

60g Parmesan, grated

60g Gruyére cheese, grated

60g white breadcrumbs

300g macaroni pasta

800ml full-fat milk

200ml double cream

75g butter

75g plain flour

1 rounded teaspoon Dijon mustard

¼ teaspoon cayenne or chilli powder

1 teaspoon butter

5 tablespoons full-fat milk

250g cream cheese

Serves 4

What you do

1 Mix 40g of the cheddar and one-third of the Parmesan into the breadcrumbs. Toss the rest of the cheeses together and set aside. Heat the oven to 190°C/Fan 170°C/Gas 5.

2 Put a pan of water on to boil. Tip the macaroni into the boiling water, cook according to the pack instructions, stirring occasionally to stop it sticking. Whilst this is cooking, start the sauce.

3 Warm the milk and cream in a saucepan. In another pan, melt the butter then stir in the flour. Cook for 1 minute, stirring, then take off the heat. Pour in one-third of the warm milk/cream and beat well with a whisk until smooth – it is quite thick at this stage. Add another third – it may go a bit lumpy, but keep beating well and it will go smooth again.

Pour in the final third of milk/cream and keep beating until smooth.

4 Next, fill your kettle and bring to the boil. When the macaroni is done, tip it into a colander in your sink and pour over the boiled water, then add a teaspoon of butter and stir through; this will keep it separate. Put the pan of sauce back on the heat and cook, stirring, until thickened and smooth.

5 Lower the heat and simmer for about 5 minutes until glossy, stirring every now and then. Remove from the heat and stir in the cheese, mustard, and cayenne/chilli powder and, at this point, add 5 tablespoons of milk to loosen the sauce slightly. Season to your taste.

6 Add the cooked macaroni to the sauce, mix well and tip into a buttered gratin dish. Blob the cream cheese over the surface then cover with the breadcrumb and cheese mixture.

7 Pop in the oven and bake for about 25-30 minutes until beginning to bubble around the edges and the topping goes golden.

Breathe in!

Creole Jambalaya

Ingredients

4 free-range chicken thighs, skin on

4 free-range chicken drumsticks, skin on

1 tablespoon olive oil

1 teaspoon sea salt

1 teaspoon cayenne/chilli powder

½ teaspoon ground black pepper

1 teaspoon sugar (for the rub)

300g good-quality smoked sausage, such as andouille or Polish garlic sausage, cut into 1cm thick slices

1 large onion, peeled and roughly chopped

1 green pepper, deseeded and roughly chopped

1 red pepper, deseeded and roughly chopped

4 sticks celery, trimmed, peeled, and roughly chopped

2 bay leaves

4 sprigs fresh thyme

6 cloves garlic, peeled and thinly sliced

1-2 fresh red chillies, deseeded and finely chopped

400g tinned chopped tomatoes

1 tablespoon sundried tomato paste

1 teaspoon sugar (for the sauce)

1.5L organic chicken stock

700g long grain rice

16-20 raw king prawns, peeled and deveined

1 handful fresh curly parsley, chopped

Serves 4

What you do

1 Rub the chicken all over with olive oil. Make a little rub with the sea salt, cayenne pepper, sugar and black pepper and sprinkle all over the joints.

2 Pour a couple of tablespoons of oil into a large casserole-type pan and brown the chicken pieces and sliced sausage over a medium heat. Remove from the pan with a slotted spoon and place on a plate.

3 Add the onion, peppers and celery as well as the bay, thyme and a pinch of salt and pepper. Stir-fry on a medium heat for 10-12 minutes, stirring every now and again. If any sticking occurs in the pan, add a couple of tablespoons of water to dissolve; this will add great flavour.

4 Once the vegetables have softened, add the garlic and chillies, stir-fry for a minute, then add the tinned tomatoes, tomato paste, sugar and chicken stock. Bring to the boil, then reduce the heat to give a slow simmer.

5 Add the chicken and sausage back into the pan, pop the lid on and simmer for 40-45 minutes. When you can pull the meat off the bone and shred it easily, the chicken's ready.

6 Add the rice, stir in, and replace the lid.

7 Give it a stir every few minutes, scraping the goodies off the bottom of the pan as you go. Let it cook for about 15-20 minutes until the rice is perfectly cooked.

8 Stir in the prawns and enough water to give a porridge consistency. Put the lid back on and cook for another 3-4 minutes, chop the parsley and garnish before serving.

This is a fab one-pot dish with a lovely garlicky flavour running through it. We just loved this served with the cheesy cornbread.

Cheesy Cornbread

Ingredients

125g butter, melted

1 small onion, finely chopped

125g corn cakes, processed to a powder

300g plain flour

1 tablespoon sugar

2 teaspoons baking powder

1½ teaspoons sea salt

150ml natural yoghurt

150ml whole milk

2 medium free-range eggs, beaten

1 medium red chilli, deseeded and finely chopped

125g extra mature cheddar, grated

Serves 4-6

What you do

1 Put 1 tablespoon of the melted butter in a small pan over a low heat. Add the onion and leave to cook for 8-10 minutes until soft and lightly golden. Set aside to cool a little.

2 Tip all the dry ingredients into a large bowl. Stir together the yoghurt, milk and eggs and then mix with the dry ingredients until smooth.

3 Preheat the oven to 200°C/Fan 180°C/Gas 6.

4 Add the chilli to the mixture along with most of the cheese, the cooked onions and all the melted butter. Stir until well combined.

5 Spoon the mixture into a greased and lined 23cm (9in) cake or 1lb loaf tin and smooth over the surface

with a spoon.

6 Cook in the preheated oven for 30-35 minutes until golden on top; insert the point of a knife in the middle – it should come out clean when cooked through. Then sprinkle over the leftover cheese and return to the oven for 5-10 minutes until golden and cooked through. Leave in the tin for a couple of minutes then turn out, cut into triangles, and serve warm with the jambalaya and a dollop of soured cream.

During lockdown we couldn't source any polenta, so I came up with the idea of blitzing a load of corn cakes (like rice cakes but made of corn). They not only worked perfectly, but the flavour and texture was so much better! Now the secret's out. We love it toasted and topped with poached Buford Brown eggs and spicy tomatoes – yum!

Moroccan
Bundle & Middle
Eastern Bundle

Lamb Tagine

Ingredients

1kg trimmed weight of lamb neck fillet, shoulder, or cushion

3 tablespoons sunflower oil

2 medium red onions, peeled and cut into thin wedges

2 large cloves garlic, grated

750ml chicken or vegetable stock

Spices

4 teaspoons cumin seeds and 4 teaspoons coriander seeds, dry roasted in a pan and ground in a spice grinder

1 teaspoon Kashmiri chilli powder

1 heaped teaspoon turmeric

1 teaspoon sea salt

½ teaspoon ground black pepper

¼ teaspoon sugar

¼ teaspoon saffron

1 large cinnamon stick

2 preserved lemons, pips removed and finely chopped

150g ready-to-eat prunes or apricots

125g soft pitted dates

50g pistachio, chopped (optional)

1 teaspoon rosewater

1 heaped teaspoon cornflour

2 tablespoons fresh chopped coriander to finish

Serves 4

What you do

1 Mix all the spices together apart from the cinnamon and saffron. Add 1 teaspoon sea salt, ½ teaspoon ground black pepper and ¼ teaspoon sugar. Sprinkle a third of the mix all over the meat, cover and leave to mingle for 1 hour.

2 Preheat your oven to 180°C/Fan 160°C/Gas 4.

③ Heat 1 tablespoon of the oil in a large skillet or good frying pan and cook the lamb in batches, browning all over; you may need a little more oil as you go. With a slotted spoon, remove into a tagine or a casserole dish with a lid (or cover tightly with foil).

④ Heat the remaining oil in the same dish over a medium heat and fry the onions for about 10 minutes or until softened and lightly coloured. Stir in the garlic, cinnamon stick and the remaining spice mix and cook for 1 minute, stirring to prevent sticking. Pour in the chicken or vegetable stock and stir through, then add the saffron and preserved lemon. Bring to a simmer and pour over the lamb, cover, and cook in the oven for 1 hour.

⑤ Next, carefully remove the dish from the oven and stir in the prunes/apricots, dates and half the pistachios (if using), cover

and return to the oven. Cook for a further 30 minutes or until the lamb is very tender.

⑥ Mix the cornflour with a tablespoon of water and the rosewater, stir through the tagine to thicken slightly, cook for a further 5 minutes and remove from the oven.

⑦ Serve with the remaining chopped pistachios and coriander.

You can make a seasonal veggie version of this using a selection of your favourite vegetables. Pre-roast to give them colour and then use all the same ingredients, but vegetable stock, of course. It will take less time to cook, about 45 minutes.

Rice and Lentil Pilaf

Ingredients

2 tablespoons olive oil

1 medium onion, peeled and finely chopped

½ teaspoon cumin seeds

½ teaspoon ground allspice

⅛ teaspoon ground cloves

4 green cardamom pods, bashed

2 bay leaves

1 cinnamon stick

300g basmati rice, washed

100g brown lentils, pre-cooked (you can cook these from raw in the stock, just check the time needed to cook them completely and work out when to add the rice, which takes 10-15 minutes)

700ml vegetable stock

1 teaspoon sea salt

¼ teaspoon saffron

50g toasted, flaked almonds

Serves 4

What you do

1 Heat a large pan, add the olive oil and the onions, cook until soft and lightly golden. Stir in the cumin, allspice, clove, cardamom, bay leaves, cinnamon stick, rice and cooked lentils. Cook for 2 minutes, then pour in the stock, sea salt and saffron and bring to the boil.

2 Reduce the heat to a simmer. Cover with a lid and cook for about 10-15 minutes until the rice has absorbed the stock. Turn the heat off and add the toasted almonds.

3 Cover and rest for 10 minutes before serving.

Lamb Kibbeh

Ingredients

Kibbeh dough

1 small onion, peeled and grated finely

1¼ teaspoons sea salt

1 level teaspoon ground allspice

1 level teaspoon ground cinnamon

½ teaspoon black pepper

275g fine bulgar wheat

450g lean minced lamb

3-4 tablespoons iced water

Stuffing

3 tablespoons olive oil

45g pine nuts (or almonds/pistachios)

2 medium-sized onions, peeled and finely chopped

150g lean minced lamb

½ teaspoon ground cinnamon

1 teaspoon sea salt

1 tablespoon of pomegranate molasses

½ tablespoon thick Greek yoghurt

Cooking

Sunflower oil

Serves 4

What you do

1 First, make the kibbeh dough by placing the onion in a bowl and mixing with the salt, allspice, cinnamon, and pepper. Rinse the bulgar and squeeze out any excess water; I use a tea towel to do this.

2 Add to the onions and mix thoroughly.

3 Add the meat and work into the bulgar, adding a little iced water at a time to create a smooth dough.

To make the filling, heat ½ tablespoon of oil in a frying pan, add the nuts of your choice and sauté until golden brown. Remove and drain on kitchen paper. Add more oil to the pan and add the onion, cooking until super soft and pale golden. Add the meat and cook until it changes colour. Sprinkle with cinnamon and salt and stir well.

④ Return the nuts to the pan and stir in the pomegranate molasses and yoghurt.

⑤ To shape the kibbeh, wet your hands with cold water, divide the mixture into 8 medium egg-sized portions. Roll each into an egg shape with your hands, using the iced water to help mould them and seal any cracks. Push your thumb in at one end and press outward, turning as you do this to form a cavity. Spoon the cooked mixture into the hollow, press it in and then seal over with the dough.

⑥ To cook the kibbeh, heat 3 inches/7.5cm of sunflower oil in a wide pan and fry in batches until golden all over; this should take about 8 minutes. Drain on kitchen paper. Eat them hot or cold at room temperature.

So many of our customers fell in love with our salads; this was the most popular and is delicious with just about anything.

Orange, Carrot, Pickled Onion and Mint Salad

Ingredients

Pickled onions

1 small red onion, peeled, halved and super thinly sliced

1 tablespoon white wine vinegar

½ teaspoon sugar

Salad

300g carrots, peeled and coarsely grated

2 large oranges, rind removed and segmented (reserve any juice that escapes for the dressing)

3 sprigs mint, leaves shredded

Fresh ground cinnamon to sprinkle

Dressing

3 tablespoons lemon juice

¼ teaspoon sea salt

2 teaspoons sugar

1 teaspoon orange flower water

Serves 4

What you do

1 Place the sliced onion in a bowl, add the vinegar and sugar, stir through, cover and pop in the fridge while you make the salad.

2 Put the grated carrot in a mixing bowl, add the orange, half the mint and cinnamon and mix through. Cover and pop in the fridge.

3 To make the dressing, simply mix the reserved orange juice, lemon juice, orange flower water, sea salt and sugar. Chill this until ready to serve. To serve, pour the dressing over the orange and carrot and mix through, then decant into a serving dish. Drain the pickled onion, scatter over the top and finish with the remaining mint.

So many people have asked for this recipe. It is a beautiful salad to look at and the taste is just perfectly refreshing, great with the kibbeh and so many other spicy dishes.

Desserts

Key Lime Pie

Ingredients

Base

300g biscuits, such as digestive, ginger snaps or hobnobs

150g unsalted butter, melted

Filling

125g dark chocolate, melted

1 x 379g tin condensed milk

3 medium free-range eggs, separated

4 limes zest, plus 125ml lime juice

To finish

300ml double cream

1 teaspoon icing sugar

1 tablespoon lime zest

25g dark chocolate, coarsely grated

Serves 4-6

What you do

1 Heat the oven to 160°C/Fan 140°C/Gas 3.

2 Break up the biscuits of your choice into a food processor and pulse to form a nice crumb. Mix with the melted butter and press into the base and up the sides of a buttered 22cm loose-based tart tin.

3 Bake in the oven for 10 minutes. Remove and cool.

4 Pour the melted chocolate into the base and spread out.

5 Put 3 medium egg yolks in a large bowl and whisk for a minute with electric whisk. Pour in the condensed milk and whisk for 3 minutes, then add the finely grated zest and lime juice and whisk again for 3 minutes.

6 Whisk the egg whites to soft peaks and fold into the mixture. Pour the filling into the biscuit case, pop into the oven and bake for 15-20 minutes or until set and firm to the touch.

7 Remove and cool, then chill for at least 3 hours or overnight in the fridge. When you are ready to serve, remove the pie from the tin and ease onto a serving plate.

8 To decorate, softly whip 300ml of double cream and the icing sugar together.

9 Dollop onto the top of the pie and finish with the extra lime zest and the grated chocolate.

An American classic with a twist of chocolate, inspired by a sweet my grandparents sold in their shop in the 70s – chocolate limes – sour candy on the outside with a chocolate centre. There's a blister forming on my tongue just thinking about it!

Chocolate Cheesecake with Praline Crumb

Ingredients

Base

125g unsalted butter, melted (plus a little extra for buttering the tin)

300g dark chocolate digestive or hobnob biscuits

Cheesecake

500g dark chocolate

300g whipped double cream

1 dessertspoon lemon juice

450g full-fat cream cheese

50g icing sugar

25g cocoa powder

25g Horlicks, Ovaltine, or a tablespoon of malt extract

Topping

2 tablespoons chocolate popping candy or coarsely grated dark chocolate

1 tablespoon pistachios, chopped

Serves 8

What you do

1 For the base, butter and line a 23cm spring-form cake tin.

2 Break the biscuits of your choice into a food processor and pulse to a fine crumb. Pour in the melted butter and pulse to combine.

3 Tip the biscuit mixture into the tin and press down firmly with the back of a spoon. Cover and chill in the fridge.

4 Next, make the cheesecake by melting the chocolate over a pan of gently simmering water. Remove and set aside to cool.

5 Using a hand whisk mix the cream, lemon juice, cream cheese, icing sugar, malted milk drink powder or malt extract and cocoa powder until smooth. Add the mixture to the chocolate bowl, stirring until well combined. Spoon the dark chocolate mixture onto the biscuit base and smooth over the top. Chill overnight.

6 To serve, ease the cheesecake onto a serving plate or cake stand.

7 Top with the popping candy or chocolate and pistachios.

This indulgent dessert answers all your chocolate needs, with popping candy to excite the palette.

Rose Meringue with Summer Fruits

Ingredients

5 eggs, whites only

275g caster sugar

75g ground almonds

1 teaspoon rose water

Topping

500ml double cream

2 tablespoons sifted icing sugar

1 teaspoon vanilla essence

400g mixed summer fruits
e.g. strawberries, raspberries,
blueberries etc.

200ml fruit sauce – make with 300g
frozen summer fruits and 3 rounded
tablespoons of sugar boiled together
and blitzed with a stick blender.
Then pass through a sieve into a
bowl. Stir in ½ teaspoon rosewater.

Serves 6-8

What you do

1 Preheat the oven to 160°C/Fan
140°C/Gas 3. Line a baking sheet
with non-stick baking parchment.

2 Beat the egg whites in a clean
bowl until stiff peaks have formed.

3 Tip in half the sugar and beat
again until stiff peaks are formed
once more. Using a metal spoon,
deftly fold in the remaining sugar a
spoonful at a time, followed by the
almonds and rosewater.

4 Tip the meringue onto the
lined sheet and spread it out quite
roughly to a 20cm circle. Cook
for 20 minutes, then reduce the
temperature to 140°C/Fan 120°C/

Gas 1 and bake for a further 40 minutes. Let the meringue cool in the oven with the door ajar or on the side, as you wish.

5 Whip the cream, icing sugar and vanilla until soft peaks form. Lightly ripple through 2 tablespoons of the fruit sauce.

6 Place the meringue on a serving plate or stand and spoon the whipped cream liberally over the top.

7 Slice the strawberries in a random manner, mix with the berries and pile on top of the cream. Drizzle with some of the fruit sauce and serve any remaining sauce at the table.

This was inspired by my late mum's garden; we had an extensive fruit and vegetable garden and lots of colourful flowerbeds. The highlights from both were the plump summer fruits and the perfumed roses. This was one of her favourite desserts.

Salted Bourbon and Caramel Pudding

Ingredients

For the sponge

250g ready-to-eat prunes or apricots

250ml boiled water

1 teaspoon bicarbonate of soda

80g butter, softened, plus a little for buttering a baking tin

2 tablespoons molasses or black treacle

80g dark muscovado sugar

2 large free-range eggs

175g plain flour

2 teaspoons baking powder

Salted caramel sauce

160g salted butter

325g dark muscovado sugar

1½ tablespoons molasses or black treacle

50ml Bourbon (optional)

225ml double cream

½ teaspoon sea salt

Serves 6-8

What you do

1 Preheat the oven to 180°C/Fan 160°C/Gas 4 and lightly butter a brownie-style tin or dish.

2 Put the chopped prunes/apricots, boiling water, and bicarbonate of soda into a bowl, stir through and then leave for 10 minutes.

3 Meanwhile make the sponge, cream the butter and molasses/

black treacle together in a stand mixer or use a hand whisk, until smooth. Add the sugar and mix again, then add one egg, once combined, add the other and keep whisking. Slowly whisk in the flour and baking powder until you have a smooth batter.

4 Using a spatula, stir the soaked prunes/apricots, pressing them against the bowl to squash them slightly, then pour the mixture into the batter and mix well.

5 Pour and scrape into your prepared dish or tin and bake for 30-35 minutes, or until the point of a knife comes out clean.

6 Meanwhile make the sauce by melting the butter, muscovado sugar and molasses/treacle over a low heat in a heavy-based pan.

7 Once the butter has melted, stir in the molasses, Bourbon if using, cream and sea salt and keep stirring while it bubbles and thickens

slightly, about 5 minutes, remove from the heat.

8 Once the sponge is cooked, remove from the oven and prick all over with a skewer or cocktail stick, pour one-third of the sauce over the top to soak in, pour the rest in a jug and serve on the side.

9 Leave to stand for 20-30 minutes, serve with whipped cream, crème fraiche or ice-cream.

This is our twist on the well known sticky toffee pudding. Apricots and prunes are lovely and slightly less sweet in the sponge, so you can indulge in more sauce!

Limoncello Meringue Pie

Ingredients

Base

300g gingernut or digestive biscuits

125g melted unsalted butter

1 teaspoon lemon zest

1 tablespoon caster sugar

Filling

3 tablespoons cornflour

100g golden caster sugar

100ml lemon juice and the zest of 2 lemons

150ml water

100ml limoncello

85g butter

3 large egg yolks, plus 1 whole egg

Italian Meringue

200g caster sugar

75ml water

4 large egg whites

Serves 6-8

What you do

1 First, make the base by breaking up the biscuits of your choice into a food processor and pulse to form a nice crumb. Mix with the melted butter, lemon zest and sugar and press into the base and up the sides of a buttered 22cm loose-based tart tin.

2 Bake in the oven at 180°C/ Fan 160°C/Gas 4 for 10 minutes. Remove and cool.

3 Next, make the filling. Mix the cornflour, sugar, and lemon zest in a pan. Gradually stir in the lemon juice then 150ml water. Bring to a simmer, stirring constantly, and bubble for a couple of minutes until thickened and smooth.

4 Remove from the heat and beat in the butter a little at a time until melted and combined. Beat the egg yolks and whole egg together and stir into the pan, put back onto a low/medium heat, keep stirring for a few minutes, until thickened. Take off the heat then stir in the limoncello.

5 Cool then pour into the biscuit case. Chill for 45 minutes.

6 To make the meringue, put the sugar in a heavy-based pan with 75ml water. Heat gently until the sugar has dissolved, then bring to the boil until the temperature reaches 120°C on a sugar thermometer.

7 Whilst the sugar is dissolving, whisk the egg whites in a large bowl to firm peaks, then slowly pour in the syrup in a thin stream, whisking all the time. Keep whisking for a few minutes until the meringue has cooled. Spoon blobs on top of the lemon filling or fill a piping bag and pipe onto the top.

8 Finish the meringue with a blowtorch to give a light golden effect, or place under a preheated grill.

9 Serve with a shot of limoncello straight from the freezer – delish!

This recipe is for Annmarie, one of our lovely customers who really pushed me to do this book. She makes a wonderful limoncello and we used it to make this dessert. There was enough left over to enjoy with it. Thank you, Annmarie!

Annmarie's Limoncello

Ingredients

375ml vodka

5 medium unwaxed lemons

750ml water

550g white sugar

What you do

1 Wash and clean the lemons with a vegetable brush to remove any wax or pesticides and pat them dry.

2 Using a potato peeler, remove all the lemon rinds from the lemons and try not to get any white pith on the rind.

3 Place the lemon rinds in a kilner jar with the clear alcohol. Seal the jar and put in a dark cupboard. Shake it once a day. On the eighth day, remove the rind from the alcohol and discard.

4 In a large saucepan, make a simple syrup by combining the water with the sugar. Let it simmer 'fast' for 15 minutes. Let the syrup cool to room temperature then add the now yellow, alcohol mixture.

5 You are now finished, bottle up and place in the freezer and it is ready to drink straight away!

Baked
Goodies

Spicy Sausage and Chorizo Rolls

Ingredients

Filling

1 tablespoon olive oil

1 small onion, peeled and finely chopped

1 teaspoon grated garlic or garlic granules

1 dessertspoon medium curry powder

600g good-quality sausage meat or peel some cracking sausages

100g chorizo sausage, finely chopped

100g fresh breadcrumbs

1 large free-range egg

1 dessertspoon mango chutney

Wrap

1 x 500g block puff pastry

1 tablespoon Dijon mustard

50g strong cheddar cheese

1 egg, beaten, with a drop of milk

Serves 8

What you do

1 Heat the oil in a frying pan set over a medium heat, add the onion and cook for 8-10 minutes until softened and golden. Stir in the garlic and cook for 1 minute, then stir in the curry powder and cook for another minute, adding 2 tablespoons of water to avoid it sticking to the pan. Transfer to a large bowl and leave to cool.

2 Add the sausage meat, chorizo, breadcrumbs, egg, and mango chutney to a bowl with the spicy onion and mix well.

3 Preheat the oven to 200°C/Fan 180°C/Gas 6.

4 Cut the block of pastry in half and roll each out into a large rectangle, approximately 10" x 5". Brush each rectangle with half of the mustard and sprinkle each with half of the cheese.

5 Halve the sausage mix and lay each half in a fat sausage shape along the long edge of one of the pastry strips. Brush the opposite edge with some of the beaten egg and milk.

6 Tightly roll up the meat in the pastry, finishing with the joint underneath. Press lightly to seal the joint.

7 Make 4 diagonal cuts through the pastry along the top of each roll.

This recipe is dedicated to Will, who has never really got over his first experience of eating them. Enjoy, Will!

8 Brush all over with the egg and cut each roll into 4 equal sausage rolls.

9 Space the rolls out on a parchment-lined baking sheet and bake in the oven for 30-35 minutes until golden, crispy, and cooked through.

Little Chicken and Ham Pies

Ingredients

Pastry
300g plain flour

130g butter

½ teaspoon sea salt

Dijon mustard

Filling
150g soft, cooked onion (see the sausage roll recipe on 154, but cooking the onion only, no spices)

1 tablespoon fresh chopped herbs – e.g. thyme, parsley, rosemary

450g chicken thigh meat (boneless, skinless, and trimmed)

250g cooked ham, shredded

1 large egg

100g fresh white breadcrumbs

4 teaspoons chutney or pickle

Beaten egg and milk for brushing

Makes 4 mini pies

What you do

1 First, make the pastry by sifting the flour into a large mixing bowl, cut in the butter and rub in with your fingertips until the mixture resembles fine breadcrumbs. Stir in the salt, then add 4-6 tablespoons of chilled water. Stir through and then push into a firm dough. Knead the dough briefly and gently on a floured surface.

2 Wrap in cling film and chill while preparing the filling.

3 Next, make the filling by simply popping everything into a mixing bowl apart from the chutney/pickle. Mix well.

4 Heavily butter and then flour 4 muffin tins, tapping out the excess (you can make 1 large 6" pie in a cake mould).

5 Divide the pastry into 4 larger balls and 4 smaller balls – roll out 4 x 7" rounds with the larger portions and 4 x 3" from the smaller rounds.

6 Line the prepared moulds with the larger rounds, gently pressing into place and flattening the folds of pastry. Brush the inside of the pies with Dijon mustard. Half fill with the chicken and ham mix, add a teaspoon of chutney/pickle and top with the remaining filling.

7 Bring the edges of the pastry in and brush over with egg wash.

8 Pop a lid on top of each and brush with egg wash. Use the handle of a teaspoon to make a crosscut in the centre of each lid.

9 Bake on a baking tray at 180°C/ Fan 160°C/Gas 4 for 35-40 minutes until golden and any juices escaping run clear. Remove from the oven, cool for 10-15 minutes and then run a dinner knife carefully around the inside edge to free the pies and lift them out.

It has to be said that these are a firm favourite with our gentlemen customers.

Fudge and Pecan Cookies

Ingredients

200g self-raising flour

200g plain flour

½ teaspoon sea salt

¼ teaspoon grated nutmeg

½ teaspoon cinnamon

175g unsalted butter, melted

200g soft dark brown sugar

100g caster sugar

2 medium free-rage eggs

50g pecans, roughly chopped

50g fudge, chopped into small cubes

Makes 16 cookies

What you do

1 Preheat your oven to 200°C/Fan 180°C/Gas 6.

2 Line 2 baking sheets with parchment paper.

3 Sift the 2 flours into a large mixing bowl and stir in the sea salt, nutmeg, and cinnamon.

4 Add the soft brown and caster sugar to the melted butter in a saucepan and mix well. Cool slightly.

5 Break the eggs into a smaller bowl and whisk together, then beat into the butter and sugar mixture until smooth.

6 Pour the sugar and egg mixture into the flour and mix with a spatula, then use an electric whisk to combine fully.

7 Divide the dough into 16 balls and flatten 8 of them on each baking sheet.

8 Stud the tops with the pecan and fudge pieces.

9 Bake in the oven for 10 minutes; the cookies will be soft when you take them out.

10 Leave to cool on the trays, then transfer onto a rack to cool completely.

We had such fun trying out different recipes for our cookies. This came out on top; we hope you agree.

Quotes from our customers

'Delicious dishes from around the world... from spicy tagines to creamy lasagne and fish pie, Angela and Olivia's 'specials' have become the culinary highlight of the week.'
Jenny Longhurst

'We love Angela and Olivia's Asian dishes, as they have the right amount of spice... just like them!'
David and Anne Brooks

'During lockdown, Friday was the highlight of the week, collecting goodies cooked by Angela and Olivia, closely followed by an email with the next week's menu. The food was delicious, with a choice of three different dishes every week, each one cooked to perfection.'
Jocelyn Price

'We decided to order a 'Bundle' from Angela and Olivia. Wow, we were blown away with the fish curry and thus we were 'hooked' (no pun). We looked forward to another delicious dish every week; in fact, it became the highlight of our week!'
Andrew and Gaynor Gretton

'If Michelin stars are the means to grade restaurants on their quality, then Angela and Olivia's 'weekly goodies' are the standard by which all other takeaway providers should be measured.'
Will Davies

Dedication

To all of us!

Especially my girl, who rose to the challenge of working with her mum. Together, we turned a real challenge into something we love.

Thanks

To our customers – From the bottom of our hearts, thank you! You were our reason to continue the good work at the School and we have had such fun preparing, making and baking and seeing you all from a distance.

To Huw – Such a creative soul who always reflects the essence of what we are trying to achieve in his images.

To Pamela – Thank you for being so amazing throughout this strange and difficult time and always being there for us all.

To my team – I love you all and miss you so much! Thanks to Lady Susan and Lady Carole for their input over the past months.

To my brother Nigel and his team (Fayebe, you are a darling!) at Castle Dairies for sponsoring all the butter that literally runs through nearly all our recipes. The Traditional Welsh Salted and Unsalted are such a pure and delicious ingredient!

To Matt Fresh – For making us laugh and for being such a great support. I know it has been so challenging, but you are made of the right stuff!

To our suppliers – Thank you, guys, for keeping the supply chain going – Jonathan at Ashtons with all that beautiful seafood and John and Del at The Black and White Pig Co for your meaty ingredients.

Delicious Bundles – Recipes from Our Kitchen to Yours
Angela Gray's Cookery School
Published in Great Britain in 2020 by Graffeg Limited.

Written by Angela Gray copyright © 2020.
Food photography by Huw Jones copyright © 2020.
Food styling by André Moore.
Designed and produced by Graffeg Limited copyright © 2020.

Graffeg Limited, 24 Stradey Park Business Centre, Mwrwg Road, Llangennech, Llanelli, Carmarthenshire, SA14 8YP, Wales, UK. Tel: 01554 824000. www.graffeg.com.

Angela Gray is hereby identified as the author of this work in accordance with section 77 of the Copyrights, Designs and Patents Act 1988.

A CIP Catalogue record for this book is available from the British Library.

ISBN 9781912213566

1 2 3 4 5 6 7 8 9